THE MORE EXCELLENT WAY.

CHAPTER I.

I am the way, the truth, and the life:—Jesus. (John 14: 6).

But covet earnestly the best gifts: and yet shew I unto you a more excellent way.—Paul. (1 Cor. 12: 31).

To find the more excellent way and walk therein is to have the greatest blessing possible of attainment by man, for the reason that it leads to everlasting life.

"Strait is the gate, and narrow is the way, which leadeth unto life, and few there be that find it."—Matt. 7: 14.

If the people whose hearts are "failing them for fear," and whose minds are filled with "perplexity," could but realize, that in the more, or as we may say, the most excellent way, there is a remedy for every ill, a healing balm for every wound, a solace for every grief, a comfort for every sorrow, and, above all, life—everlasting life—in the world to come, how infinitely better might their condition be. But alas, how few are able to do so!

"Wide is the gate, and broad is the way, that leadeth unto destruction, and many there be which go in thereat."—Matt. 7: 13.

The voice of the "Good Shepherd" is heard and heeded by few indeed. The disturbed condition of the religious world, the many conflicting theories that are being zealously advocated by a multitude of would-be teachers; the low standard of morality and spirituality, and the lack of faith and confidence in God and in Christ, in the more popular churches; the direct attacks upon the teaching of Jesus as set forth in the New Testament, by avowed infidels, agnostics *et al.*, all add to the difficulties of the honest in heart, in their search for, and their efforts to walk in, the "more excellent way." The straightness of this way makes it still more difficult for those who are accustomed to walk in crooked paths, to follow therein. The people seem to be wholly engrossed in a mad, blind pursuit of earthly pleasures; and these are so unsatisfactory, so utterly incapable of bringing happiness to the perplexed and troubled soul, that there is absolutely "no peace for the wicked," as saith the prophet. That which he thought would give pleasure, gives pain instead. The rose, that with anxious longings he seeks to pluck, and from which he fondly hopes to breathe the fragrance of contentment and joy, is instantly blighted, leaving nothing in his eager hand but the hidden thorn. The exquisite pleasures for which his soul constantly longs are illusive and evasive, always in some distant place or in the vague and uncertain "tomorrow." Like the fabled sack of gold at the end of the rainbow, they cannot quite be obtained—always a little farther on. And why?

"Because my people hath forgotten me, they have burned incense to vanity, and they have caused them to stumble in their ways from the ancient paths, to walk in paths, in a way not cast up."—Jer. 18: 15.

It is only in "the way," the "straight way," the "more excellent," yea, the *most* excellent way, that the true happiness for which weary, troubled souls are constantly longing, can be found. Hence, the prophet says:

"Thus saith the Lord, Stand ye in the ways, and see, and ask for the old paths, where is the good way, and walk therein, and ye shall find rest for your souls."—Jer. 6: 16.

Glorious promise! "Rest for your souls." How the heart of the wayworn pilgrim rejoices in the very thought! Rest, sweet rest! "They shall rest from their labors and their works do follow them." It falls upon the head of the weary soul like the dews of heaven upon the drooping flower. What would one not give for a full and comprehensive knowledge of this "good way," so that he might walk therein? What a blessing to the human family, if all would heed the command to "ask for the old paths, where is the good way, and walk therein," until in every land, among all people, there should be heard the glad refrain, "Peace on earth, good will to men."

It is very important to know something about the way, so that we may be able to so walk that we shall never be found in the broad way; and it shall be our purpose to place the two ways—the straight and narrow, and the broad way—before you in such a clear and logical manner that none of you need make a mistake. To this end may the Lord bless with his Holy Spirit, the Comforter, all those who read, as well as the writer, that all may be mutually benefited in our search for light and knowledge concerning this most momentous question, "The more excellent way."

It will not be disputed, I think, that such terms as "the way," "the good way," "the way of life," "the more excellent way," are synonymous in meaning with the gospel of Christ; howbeit, the latter term, as used in the text at the head of this article, has a primary meaning of a more specific nature, which we shall probably notice at some length later on.

The author of the book of Romans says:

"I am not ashamed of the gospel of Christ: for it is the power of God unto salvation to every one that believeth; to the Jew first, and also to the Greek. For therein is the righteousness of God revealed from faith to faith: as it is written, the just shall live by faith."—Rom. 1: 16, 17.

In the testimony of St. Mark we read:

"Go ye into all the world, and preach the gospel to every creature. He that believeth and is baptized shall be saved; but he that believeth not shall be damned."—Mark 16: 15, 16.

This testimony clearly sets forth the fact that the gospel is that by which or through which God proposes to exercise his power to save those who believe it, unless, for some reason, they should believe in vain; for elsewhere we read:

"Moreover, brethren, I declare unto you the gospel which I preached unto you, and which ye have received, and wherein ye stand; by which also ye are saved, if ye keep in memory what I preached unto you, unless ye have believed in vain."— 1 Cor. 15: 1, 2.

Nothing can be clearer than the fact that the gospel of Christ is the means by which salvation, or the privilege of entering into the rest "that remains for the people of God," is to be secured. Hence, Paul says: "For we which have believed do enter into rest." (Heb. 4: 3).·

As before seen, the Lord, through the prophet Jeremiah, promises rest on condition. "Stand in the ways, and see, ask for the old paths, where is the good way, and *walk therein.*" And as Paul with his Hebrew brethren had entered into rest, it follows that, somewhere along the line, they had stood in the ways, they had asked for the old paths, they had found them, had "walked therein," and in so doing had found "rest to their souls"—entered "into rest"—all because they had believed the gospel plan of salvation as taught by Jesus the Christ. This certainly was an excellent, if not "a *more* excellent way" to be saved. They had, no doubt, heard the voice of the Good Shepherd, saying:

"Come unto me all ye that labor and are heavy laden and I will give you rest."

To them this promise had been verified, because they had walked in "the way"—had believed the gospel of Christ, and had not "believed in vain."

In this way they were made free, not only from the law of

Moses, but also from sin. On this point Paul says:

"The law of the Spirit of life in Christ Jesus hath made me free from the law of sin and death."—Rom. 8: 2.

Jesus says:

"If the Son therefore shall make you free, ye shall be free indeed."—John 8: 36.

Again:

"Where is boasting then? It is excluded. By what law? of works? Nay: but by the law of faith."—Rom. 3: 27.

Thus it is seen that salvation, entrance into "rest," "freedom from "sin and death," was obtained by obedience to the gos·pel of Christ, or the "*law* of the spirit of life," or the *law* of faith, taught by Jesus and the apostles of old; and the question, What is the nature or character of this law? here suggests itself.

David answers thus:

"The law of the Lord is *perfect* converting the soul."—Ps. 19: 7.

And James, thus:

"Whoso looketh into the *perfect* law of liberty, and continueth therein, he being not a forgetful hearer, but a doer of the work, this man shall be blessed in his deed."—James 1: 25.

And Solomon:

"Every word of God is pure."—Prov. 30: 5.

It cannot be doubted that this "perfect law, referred to by both David and James, and the "pure" word of God referred to by Sol-omon, is that which the apostles were sent to all the world to teach, and which the people were required to accept, with promise of salvation for so doing; or to reject at the peril of damnation; for David says it *converts* the soul, and it is certainly converted souls, not unconverted ones, that are saved. Hence, Peter says:

"Repent ye therefore, and be converted, that your sins may be blotted out, when the times of refreshing shall come from the presence of the Lord."—Acts 3: 19.

Assuming (and it is a fair assumption) that Peter understood as well as David—just as did David—God's method of converting the soul; in other words, assuming that Peter agrees with David that it is the "law of the Lord" that converts the soul, and Peter's meaning in the above quotation is clear. He simply means that those men to whom he addressed himself, were to put themselves in touch with the law of God, and by its operations be "converted," so that "times of refreshing may come from the presence of the Lord."

He enjoins them (first) to repent, and (second) to be converted. This shows that being converted was something which they could do as well as to repent; or, putting it in another form, they could do something that would bring about the operations of the "perfect law of liberty," "the law of faith," "the law of the Spirit of life in Christ Jesus,"upon their souls, and thus be converted, and they would be saved; their sins be blotted out; and times of refreshing would come from the presence of the Lord; and in this way they would find "rest to their souls" —be freed from sin and its consequences.

"For the law of the Spirit of life in Christ Jesus hath made me free from the law of sin and death," saith Paul.   (Rom. 8: 2).

And again:

"But now being made free from sin, and become servants to God, ye have your fruit unto holiness, and the end everlasting life."—Rom. 6: 22.

Whatever he may have meant by the words, "law of sin and death," whether he was referring to the law of Moses in an exclusive sense, or to everything that produces evil, or in any way causes sin, there can be no doubt that by the words, "Law of the Spirit of life in Christ Jesus," he meant that particular moral and spiritual code, that distinctively peculiar system of faith known as the gospel, which Jesus taught while on earth, and authorized others to teach in all the world, among all nations, with promise that, "He that believeth and is baptized shall be saved," and with solemn warning that, "He that believeth [it]

not shall be damned." (See Mark 16: 15, 16).

Peter, as one of the chosen representatives of Jesus, and one who enjoyed to a great degree the Spirit of his Master, evidently understood this matter just as did Paul, as the following will show:

"Seeing ye have purified your souls [been converted], in obeying the truth through the Spirit unto unfeigned love of the brethren, see that ye love one another with a pure heart fervently: being born again [converted], not of corruptible seed, but of incorruptible, by the word of God, which liveth and abideth forever. * * * But the word of the Lord endureth forever.   And this is the word which by the gospel is preached unto you."— 1 Peter 1: 22–25.

Surely, if it was the word of the Lord "which by the gospel is preached unto you," by which those to whom Peter wrote were "born again" (and without which they could not see the kingdom of God, John 3: 3), and if by the "law of the Lord" which is perfect, David's soul was converted; and Paul's was made free from sin and its consequences by the "law of the Spirit of life in Christ Jesus," then all these terms must mean the same thing; and if this is granted, then there is no escape from the conclusion, that by each and all of them is meant the gospel of Christ, the law of faith; for, saith Peter, "This *is the word which by the* GOSPEL is preached unto you." He was one of those, too, who were told to go into all the world and "preach the gospel to every creature;" and Paul wrote, "I declare unto you the gospel which I preached unto you * * * and by which ye are saved." (1 Cor. 15:1).

Thus is clearly shown the fact that the means used by the Almighty in the conversion of the soul of the sinner is the law of the Lord, or word of God, styled by the apostle to the gentiles, "the law of faith." Any professed conversion of any soul by any other means, would, to put it in as mild a form as possible, place the one making such profession on very doubtful ground; and when it is remembered that there is no profit to be derived by gaining even the whole world at the expense of one's soul (Mark 8:36), the seriousness of occupying a doubtful position forcibly presents itself.

This life is so short that though one had the world at his command, with power to enjoy to the fullest extent all that it affords, he could not in all this be recompensed for the loss of his soul. If he has not been "born again," if his soul has not been "converted," if he has not been made free from sin and death, if it should be said to him: "Thou fool, this night shall thy soul be required of thee" (Luke 12:20); if it is said to him, "Depart from me, ye workers of iniquity;" if, Dives-like, he dies, is buried, and lifts up his eyes in torment, if he shall say, "The summer is ended the harvest is past and *my soul is not saved*" (Jer. 8:20); methinks the anguish of such a soul for one hour would cause to pass out of remembrance all the pleasures, real or imaginary, that the world had given him in life.

How important then to be right in the matter of the soul's conversion. How necessary to use the God-appointed, heaven-ordained means by which the proper conversion, the complete salvation of the soul, can be obtained. Not only should we be willing to accept God's plan in preference to any other, but we should be willing to accept a full, free and complete operation of his perfect law with us; so that our conversion shall be also full and complete, and that we may have ministered unto us, abundantly, an entrance into the everlasting kingdom of our Lord and Savior Jesus Christ; and that we may be among those who shall be presented "without spot or wrinkle or any such thing." (See 2 Peter 1:11; Eph. 5:27).

Men have "sought out many inventions" in spiritual as well as temporal things; and it is not surprising to a logical reasoner to find that *all* man-made plans and human inventions for the salvation of the race are in some respects at least in direct opposition to the plan of salvation as revealed from heaven by him who said: "I am *the way*;" and it is certain that any way opposed to, or different from that, is not the "more excellent way." Any way or plan which differs from the gospel as revealed in the Scriptures, cannot be . "more excellent" than the plan there revealed. To contend that some other is more excellent, is to contend that Jesus was not infallible and that the Bible is not to be relied upon in such matters. Who, except an avowed infidel, would make such a contention? Who indeed?

Do not be startled, kind friend, whoever you may be, when I tell you that many, who not only are not avowed infidels, but who are professors of religion, and some of them professed ministers of the gospel, *do*, though unwittingly, virtually make just such a contention. This will appear as we proceed.

The fact that there are many human plans and only *one* divine one, increases the difficulty of many who are asking in all earnestness for the old paths, and who really desire to be saved. Not that the divine plan is not plain and easy of comprehension, provided one is in such condition of mind as to be receptive of the influence of the Spirit of God. but because of the conflicting theories, to the consideration of which their minds are invited.

Since the days when it was thought by Luther, Calvin, Knox, and others to be necessary to reform the Catholic church; and when, by the Wesleys, reformation was thought to be necessary in the Episcopal church, the work of laying out plans and organizing churches has gone steadily on, each *new* way claiming to be the "good *old* way," and its votaries have been loud and constant in giving invitation to all the people to walk with them, promising them rest on condition of accepting the invitation; some have gone so far as to employ physical force in order to establish their faith when moral suasion failed.

This, it seems to me, is not the "more excellent way." The Savior says:

"My kingdom is not of this world: if my kingdom were of this world, then would my servants fight, that I should not be delivered to the Jews: but now is my kingdom not from hence." —John 18:36.

"The kingdom of heaven is not meat and drink, but righteousness and *peace* and joy in the Holy Ghost," saith Paul.

"He that believeth and is baptized," not he who is *forced* to accept in a formal way, what he does *not* really believe, "shall be saved." Nor would it better the condition of any man or people if they were forced to accept any religious theory of human origin, or suffered themselves to be led to accept it by the sophistry or ingenuity of self-appointed teachers, or by considerations of popularity, rather than to accept "the way" as set forth in the life-work and teachings of Jesus the Lord. By such a course their condition might be made worse, but not better. "I am the way," is the language of Jesus. And again he saith, "He that climbeth up some other way, the same is a thief and a robber." (John 10:1). Robber of what? Not of goods of this world, but it would be an attempted robbery of the right of Jesus to be "the way;" in other words, the right to say what is the way, to the exclusion of *all* others, men or angels.

On this point Paul bears testimony as follows:

"But though we, or an angel from heaven, preach any other gospel [way] unto you than that which we have preached unto you, let him be accursed. As we said before, so say I now again, If any man preach any other gospel [way] unto you than that [gospel or way] ye have received, let him be accursed."—Gal. 1:8, 9.

And why be accursed? Because he would be seeking to climb up some other way, and would influence others to do the same; and all such would, as we have seen, become "thieves and robbers." It belongs, I repeat, to Jesus *alone*, under the direction of the Spirit of God, his Father, to say along what lines, and through what places, pleasant or unpleasant, shall be the way of life; not even the apostles were permitted to make any changes or preach otherwise than directed of the Lord.

"I have given them the words which thou gavest me; and they have received them."—John 17:8.

Again:

"As thou [the Father] hast sent me [the Son] into the world, even so have I also sent them [the apostles] into the world."—(18th verse).

Query: How did the Father send Jesus into the world?

Answer: "For I have not spoken of myself; but the Father which sent me, he gave me a commandment, what I should say, and what I should speak. And I know that his commandment is life everlasting: whatsoever I speak therefore, even as the Father said unto me, so I speak."—John 12:49, 50.

If then Christ was sent with a commandment in his mouth what he was to "say and what he should speak," and if the apostles were sent as he was sent, they too were sent with a commandment in their mouth, what they were to say, and what they should speak. And having been thus *commanded* to teach the words Christ had received of his Father and gave to them, of course, they themselves, nor others, not even angels, were authorized to teach otherwise.

Further:

"I [God] will raise them up a Prophet from among their brethren, like unto thee [Moses], and will put my words in his mouth; and he shall speak unto them all that I shall command him. And it shall come to pass, that whosoever will not hearken unto my words which he shall speak in my name, I will *require it of him.*"—Deut. 18: 18, 19.

Thus we see that when God sends a prophet with a message to the people, the people are under obligation to hear and give proper heed to the message brought. This is true of any prophet of any age of the world; but with respect to Jesus, the Lord, it is pre-eminently so.

Peter, in an eloquent appeal to the people who came together, and stood in wonder and amazement at the sight of a man whom they had long known to be a cripple and a supplicant of alms from the people at the "gate of the temple which is called Beautiful," but who, at the commandment of Peter to "rise up and walk," was soon seen by them in the temple, "walking and praising God,"

made application of the foregoing prophecy to Jesus in this wise:

"And he shall send Jesus Christ, which before was preached unto you: whom the heaven must receive until the times of restitution of all things, which God hath spoken by the mouth of all his holy prophets since the world began. For Moses truly said unto the fathers, A prophet shall the Lord your God raise up unto you of your brethren, like unto me; him shall ye hear in all things whatsoever he shall say unto you. And it shall come to pass, that every soul, which will not hear that prophet, shall be destroyed from among the people. Yea, and all the prophets from Samuel and those that follow after, as many as have spoken, have likewise foretold of *these days.*"—Acts 3: 20-24.

The latter quotation, if anything, is stronger than the first in its condemnation of those who fail to hear the words of the prophet, who was, according to this prediction of Moses, to be raised up. Of anyone who refuses to hearken to his words, Moses says: "I [God] will require it;" whereas Peter says that every such soul "shall be destroyed from among the people," and in another place the same apostle says:

"Neither is there salvation in any other [than Jesus]: for there is none other name [than Jesus] under heaven given among men, whereby we must be saved."—Acts 4: 12.

And again, the Savior himself is on record, thus:

"He that rejecteth me, and receiveth not my words, hath one that judgeth him: the word that I have spoken, the same shall judge him in the last day."—Jno. 12: 48.

What, kind reader, do you think will be the character of such a judgment, of such a one as has rejected him, in the last day? If you hesitate, let me give you an idea from some of the words that Jesus has spoken, and by which you and I, and all the race of man shall be judged:

"Not everyone that saith unto me, Lord, Lord, shall enter into the kingdom of heaven; but he that *doeth* the will of my Father which is in heaven. Many will say unto me in that day, Lord, Lord, have we not prophesied in thy name? and in thy name have cast out devils? and in thy name done many wonderful works? And then will I profess unto them, I never knew you: depart from me, *ye that work iniquity*." (Matt. 7: 21-23). "Whosoever heareth these sayings of mine, and *doeth* them, I will liken him unto a wise man, which built his house upon a rock * * * and it fell not. And everyone that heareth these sayings of mine and *doeth them not*, shall be likened unto a foolish man, which built his house upon the sand: * * * and it fell: and great was the fall of it."—v. 24-27.

In the foregoing verses I have emphasized the words "doeth" and "doeth not," to invite particular attention to them. "Whosoever doeth these sayings" of Jesus was to be accounted wise, and everyone that did not do them was to be likened unto a foolish man. Let us remember that "these sayings," *all* the "sayings," "words" of Jesus are what we shall be judged by in the last day, and in that judgment we will be found guilty, or not guilty; we will be adjudged wise or foolish.

The difference in the condition of the wise and foolish is strikingly and forcefully set forth in the parable of the ten virgins, as found in the 25th chapter of Matthew:

"And the foolish said unto the wise, Give us of your oil; for our lamps are gone out. But the wise answered, saying, Not so; lest there be not enough for us and you: but go ye rather to them that sell, and buy for yourselves. And while they [the foolish] went to buy, the bridegroom came; and they that were ready [the wise] went in with him to the marriage: and the door was shut. Afterward came also the other virgins, saying, Lord, Lord, open to us. But he answered and said, Verily, I say unto you, I know you not." (v.

8–12). I quote again: "Many [who have not done the will of God and are, therefore, of the class represented by the foolish virgins, or the man who built his house upon the sand] will say unto me [Christ, the bridegroom] in that day, Lord, Lord, have we not prophesied in thy name? and in thy name cast out devils? and in thy name done many wonderful works? Then will I [in passing judgment upon them according to their works, Rev. 20: 12, and by "the word which I have spoken"] profess unto them I never knew you: depart from me, ye that work iniquity."— Matt. 7: 22, 23.

In the parable of the talents the difference in the conditions of these two classes, the wise and the foolish, the doers of the sayings of Jesus and those who do them not, is set forth thus:

"His Lord said unto him [the one who was wise enough to improve on his talents], Well done, thou good and faithful servant: thou hast been faithful over a few things, I will make thee ruler over many things: enter thou into the joy of thy Lord."— Matt. 25: 21.

And:

"His Lord answered and said unto him [the unwise, unprofitable servant], Thou wicked and slothful servant, thou knewest that I reap where I sowed not, and gathered where I have not strawed: thou oughtest there-fore to have put my money to the exchangers, and then at my coming I should have received mine own with usury. Take therefore the talent from him, * * * and cast ye the unprofitable servant into outer darkness: there shall be weeping and gnashing of teeth."—vs. 26, 27, 28, 30.

I have been thus particular to present the character and results of the judgment that will be passed in the last day upon all mankind, that the importance of *doing* the "sayings" of Jesus, and thus proving ourselves wise, may be seen, and the results of a failure so to do, may be fully understood. The importance of being right in matters of religion, cannot be overestimated.

To forsake the Lord and walk in "paths not cast up" by him, may be more pleasant, apparently so, at least, than to walk in the old paths, the "straight way," the "more excellent way;" but such a course leads one into the midst of dangers, very great indeed, yea, to certain destruction in the end. "Broad is the way" of this world, and it leads to destruction, and many are gaily walking down this broad way, heedless of the dangers that beset them on every hand. Worldly pleasures engross the minds and efforts to obtain them, engage the talents of this immense throng, and the gay and giddy world looks on with satisfaction and smiles her approbation. "Mystery Babylon"—false and corrupt religion of every kind and color, looks on the scene as if enchanted, and eagerly asks: "May *I walk with you* along this great, broad way?" And the world answers, "Yes, we shall be only too glad to have you." Soon *all* are engulfed in the busy whirl of pursuits of such things as do not satisfy, even if obtained. Such may be likened unto thoughtless children, catching butterflies for their beauty, and then carelessly, or wilfully and wickedly, crushing them, and watching them die in their hands.

Into the mouths of this class Jeremiah put these words: "The harvest is past, the summer is ended, and we are not saved." (Jer. 8:20). And John these: "And said to the mountains and rocks, Fall on us, and hide us from the face of him that sitteth on the throne, and from the wrath of the Lamb."—Rev. 6: 16.

Such will be the end of those who do not "ask for the old paths and walk therein;" who will not accept "*The way*, the truth, and the life" of the world, but who prefer the broad way of destruction instead. On the other hand those who walk in the "more excellent way," even though it be a "straight and narrow" one, will "Sing a new song, saying, Thou art worthy to take the book, and to open the seals thereof: for

thou wast slain, *and hast redeemed us to God* by thy blood, out of every kindred, and tongue, and people and nation." (Rev. 5: 9). And again: "Alleluia, salvation, and glory, and honour, and power, unto the Lord our God: * * * Let us be glad and rejoice, and give honour to him: for the marriage of the Lamb is come, and his wife hath made herself ready." (Rev. 19: 1, 7).

The reader is advised to read the whole of the 18th chapter and to the close of the 9th verse of the 19th chapter of Revelation, where will be found a vivid picture of the difference in the conditions of those who are "converted," "saved," "born again," "made free from sin and death," "entered into rest," "found rest to their souls," "builded their house [spiritual house or life work] upon a rock," "took oil in their vessels with their lamps," and withal made themselves "ready," and those to whom it shall be said: "Depart from me, ye workers of iniquity, I never knew you," and who shall say: "The summer is ended, the harvest is past, and *we are not saved.*"

It is believed that when the reader has looked upon this picture until his conception is somewhat correct, his mind will be made up as to which condition is more preferable and in which he would wish to be, and we trust he will be fully resolved to follow in the way that leads to the condition of rest—eternal life.

Any soul that realizes to any degree what it is to be saved and what it is to be lost, very naturally and with great earnestness asks, "What shall I do to be saved," "where shall I find the way that leads to life?" "Where is the old path that I may walk therein and find rest to my weary, troubled soul?"

Gently as the zephyrs of a calm summer evening; yea, softly as the gentle cadences of angel songs the answer falls upon waiting, listening ears. It comes from the lips of Him who spake as never man spake. Listen, O anxious one, whoever you may be: *"Hear and your soul shall live."* (Isa. 55: 3). Are you listening? Are you willing to hear? Then you shall hear as from the lips of the Son of God himself, *"I* am *the* way," "Come unto *me all* ye that labor and are heavy laden and *I* will give you rest."

"But," says the anxious one, "how shall I go to him? In what sense can I walk in him as *"the* way?" The answer to this question has seemed, and really has been, a very difficult one to many. I shall try to put up the guide boards along at such places as will enable any one to keep his bearings as he walks along the way. You could not walk in a meadow or in a wood until you *are in* the meadow or wood, then may you walk therein and enjoy the beauties of each, or either,

but not before. But if you stay on the outside, none of the *inside* pleasures of the meadow or wood can come to you. And this fact, self-evident and clear as it must be to all, is no more true than the fact that only those who are *in Christ* can walk in him as the way.

"Therefore if any man be in Christ, he is a new creature: old things are passed away; behold, all things are become new." (2 Cor. 5: 17).

Just as the weary traveler, foot-sore and with parched lips, leaves the dusty highway and turns into the flowery woods where winged songsters warble forth their sweetest strains, and where roses, rich with perfume and beautiful colors, bloom forth to please the eye and heart, and where fountains of cool, sparkling water burst forth to give life to everything towards which they flow; and sits himself down on a grassy plot beneath the thick, spreading branches of some friendly tree well laden with luscious fruit, may find rest to his body; so may the weary, sin-sick soul by leaving the highways of sin, the broad way that leads to death, and getting into Christ—the Christ life—find rest, yea, sweet rest in him; for saith he, "I will give you rest." And it is all free. "Whosoever will, let him come." Precious invitation! Reader, can you afford to slight it?

Many are ready, nay, anxious to come and quench the thirsting of their souls at the fountain of living water and satisfy their heart hunger by eating of the "bread from heaven" (John 6:32); but how to find the fountain, how to obtain the bread, how to get into the conditions of the Christ-life, is the puzzling question. It must be answered, and I beg of the reader not to lose sight of the importance of having the *right* answer. Remember that you can find rest to your soul in no other than "the good way."

We have seen the necessity of being in Christ; but as the mountain side against which we talk sends back the echo of our own words, so many souls, if asked to walk in Christ as the way, send back the cry, "How can we get in him that we may walk in 'the good way?' "

"Know ye not that so many of us as were baptized into his death?"—Rom. 6: 4.

"For as many of you as have been baptized into Christ have put on Christ."—Gal. 3: 27.

From the above passages it is easy to see that persons are *baptized* into Christ; and it is also clear that if a man who has been "baptized into Christ, has put on Christ," then he who has been baptized into Christ is in Christ and is, therefore, "a new creature. The converse is equally true: "For as many of you as have" *not* "been baptized into Jesus Christ have" not "put on Christ;" consequently not in Christ, therefore not "a new creature"—not converted, not in "the more excellent way" to be saved.

CHAPTER II.

In the closing paragraphs of chapter 1 we showed the necessity of getting into Christ, for we cannot walk in him unless we *are in* him; and if we are not in him we are not in the more excellent way; for he is "the way, the truth and the life." It was also shown that Paul taught the Romans, and also the Galatians, that they "were baptized into Christ.' The writer believes that it is yet a good way, a more excellent way to get into Christ. He does not believe, however, that baptism in water alone, or that Spirit baptism alone fills up the full measure of the way, but that both are necessary, together with other gospel principles, as will appear as we proceed.

But before presenting other Scriptural evidences on this line, I will here give a simple illustration which, notwithstanding its crudeness, will, I think, aid the honest investigator in his search for the way of life, and in understanding what it is to be in Christ.

Ardent Youthful is *in love.* No one would for a moment believe that he has only heard a pleasing story of the existence of some sweet Rose Mary, somewhere in the world, though he has not seen her, nor had any communication with her, nor is he sure she is alive, or ever was; but still he hopes she lives, and that some day he will be permitted to bask in her smiles, and that she will then reciprocate his love. If he is in love it is because he has some knowledge of the sweet Rose Mary who is the object of his love; and with his faith in her qualities that render her lovable in his sight, he will unite such works of honor as will satisfy all the laws of his goddess.

Thus he is in the conditions of the new environments, new life, new service, entailed by the magic word "love," and in such new life, conditions of service to his fair goddess will he patiently continue, being careful not to offend her by violation of, or rebellion against any of her laws that must shape the life of the man she weds. He no longer lives for himself nor in himself alone, but has moved out of the old condition and into the new; is, in fact, a "new creature," and occupies, relatively, a new position.

Again:

We frequently hear statements such as: "Mr. Jones or Mr. Davis is *in* politics." Every one understands what is meant by such statements. They know that Mr. Jones or Mr. Davis *believe in*, and are working with reasonable persistency to carry out the political doctrines of the party to which he belongs and has pledged himself. No one would think Mr. Jones was a democrat because he said he *believed*, though he was not quite sure—did not really know—there was such a thing in existence as the Democratic party. If he was really in politics, he would, no doubt, have a perfect knowledge of the existence of his party, and at least a partial understanding of its doctrines; and he would be expected to vote and otherwise work for its success. If he did not, he might *say* he was a Democrat ever so loud, and ever so many times, but no one would ever believe it.

Yet, strange as it may seem, when it comes to religion, when it comes to finding "the way" of which we are now in search, many arrive, or rather, jump at conclusions equally as erroneous, and say that believing in Christ as the Savior (though such believer is not sure he exists, nor has he done anything in the service of, or obedience to him; in other words, has done nothing to carry out or make successful the spiritual economy of Christ, as applicable to himself and to the world; in short, has not made a single move in the direction of doing the "sayings" of Jesus, or of obeying his gospel, save the bare profession of faith in him as the Savior of the world) will make a man a christian, or place him in Christ. Why is it that we cannot use as much wisdom in passing judgment in things spiritual or religious as in things carnal or earthly?

To be *in* politics means to be engaged in the interest of whatever form of political economy one chooses to adopt, and this engagement means the employment of both mind and body, or faith and works, in the interest of such political economy or doctrine. In like manner, to be *in* Christ means to be engaged in the interest of his "sayings," his "doctrine," his "gospel," his spiritual economy, or "law of faith," which, as we have seen, is perfect and converts the soul. And this engagement must be with all the heart, mind, soul and body. Putting it in another form, it must include an intelligent service of both soul and body, or a union of faith and works.

"For ye are bought with a price: therefore glorify God in your body, and in your spirit which are God's."—1 Cor. 6: 20.

As a man cannot be in politics by simply believing in the existence of his party, or some great party leader, and not working and voting with his party; and as a man cannot be in love by simply believing in the existence of some fair one of whom he knows nothing, and for whom he does nothing to please and satisfy, even so no man can be IN Christ who has gone no further than to believe in his existence as his Savior, or the Savior of the world, without doing something to satisfy the demands of his law. Merely saying, Lord, Lord, will not satisfy the demands nor answer the requirements.

"Ye must be born again," or from "above," saith the Savior. But how can it be done, "how can a man be born when he is old?" is the ever important question.

To be in Christ means to be in the Christ life, in the conditions of life produced by walking in his footsteps, by hearing and doing his sayings. It means to live in the environments that obtain in the highest and best sphere of spirituality; that in which Jesus Christ moved, and the ethics of which he presented to the world in the "more excellent way." It means to be raised from the low standard of earth-life to walk in the spirituality of the higher life in Christ Jesus. It means that "old things," old conditions of the lower walks of earth-life, of sinfulness and rebellion against God and his law have passed away, and "all things"—environments, conditions, laws governing us—have been changed, "have been made new." In a word it means being delivered from the "power of darkness, and translated into the kingdom of God's dear Son." (Col. 1: 13).

"For we are his workmanship, created in Christ Jesus unto good works, which God hath before ordained that we should walk in them."—Eph. 2: 10.

"Created in Christ Jesus!" Such an one is in Christ, in the conditions of the Christ life, having heard and having done the sayings of Jesus. Such an one has asked for "the old paths, where is the good way," has walked therein, has found rest to his soul, has been "converted," has been "born again." And still the question comes, "How can a man be born *when he is old?*" And inspiration is ready with the answer: "Born again' * * by the word of God, * * and this is the word, which, by the gospel, is preached unto you."

This word evidently includes all that is comprehended in the announcement of Jesus:

"My doctrine is not mine but his that sent me."—John 7: 16.

And also this:

"He that abideth in the doctrine of Christ, he hath both the Father and the Son."—2 John 9.

And again:

"And they continued steadfastly in the apostles' doctrine and fellowship, and in breaking of bread, and in prayers."—Acts 2: 42.

I presume that no one will dispute the proposition that Christ's doctrine and the apostles' doctrine were one and the same thing. Whatever then, is on record, authoritatively, as having been taught by the Savior and by the apostles, must be regarded as Christ's doctrine, the apostles' doctrine, the gospel which Jesus himself taught, and sent his apostles out to preach to all the world. And those who believed and were baptized were saved, "born again," born into the Christ life, and all this because they heard, believed, and obeyed the "word, which by the gospel was preached unto them," for thus saith Paul:

"Ye have obeyed from the heart that form of doctrine which was delivered you. Being *then* made free from sin, ye became the servants of righteousness."—Rom. 6: 17, 18.

And Peter:

"Ye have purified your souls in *obeying* the truth."—1 Peter 1: 22.

Reader, is not this the good way, "the more excellent way?" Will any other way lead you to the same happy condition of purification of soul? Nay, verily, "He that climbeth up some other way the same is a thief and a robber."

But what had those servants of righteousness believed and obeyed? What were the principles of faith and doctrine accepted by them? And what the word preached unto them and by which they were born again? And an apostolic dignitary stands ready to answer thus:

"Therefore leaving the principles of the doctrine of Christ, let us go on to perfection; not laying again the foundation of repentance from dead works, and of faith toward God, of the doctrine of baptisms, and of laying on of hands, and of resurrection of the dead, and of eternal judgment."—Heb. 6: 1-4.

Here we have a clear and succinct statement of what Paul or Barnabas, or whoever this writer was, calls "the *principles* of the doctrine of Christ;" and in the previous chapters he refers to them as the "first principles of the oracles of God," and it is clear that belief in and obedience to these "principles" of faith or doctrine, was what "purified," "converted," "saved" the souls of those who were born again by the word which was preached unto them. And this being true, it follows that this heaven-ordained plan was for them, and is for us, the more, yea, the most excellent way to be saved.

This is objected to, however, by some, and the claim is made that the principles referred to were parts of the Jewish economy under the law, and that the "hand writing of ordinances" was blotted out by Christ; and nothing is now necessary save only to have faith, and that it, alone, will purify, convert, save the soul. To the writer, this does not seem to be the "more excellent way." The principal reason for such objection is to make it appear, if possible, that baptism in water for the remission of sins, and the laying on of hands for the gift of the Holy Ghost are not essential, the one to forgiveness of sins and the other to the reception of the Holy Spirit. Many conscientiously believe that they have received and will receive a fullness of blessing and glory, who have observed neither. They think they have found an easier if not a more excellent way. No good, in their judgment, can come to them by an observance of the ordinance of baptism or of the beautiful rite of the laying on of hands. "By faith *only* sins are forgiven; by faith only we are born again, converted," say they; and, as some of old have said: "What profit is it that we have kept his ordinance?" (Mal. 3: 14). "How can baptism save? What is the use in the laying on of hands? What profit is there in either?" But if the "principles" referred to in the passage from Hebrews, are applicable to the Jewish order alone and not to the christian, then the people should not be urged to have faith or repent; for these are two of the principles mentioned, and if this passage is applicable to the Jew-

ish form of worship only, and not to the christian, then no christian is under obligation to believe or to repent. Who would take such a position as that? The Savior says: "Repent ye therefore, and believe the gospel;" and Peter says, "The Lord is willing that all should come to repentance." If Jesus Christ who announces himself to be "*the* way" "wills," nay, *commands* that men should repent, is it not getting out of "the way" to say it is not in the christian, but belongs exclusively to the Mosaic order. I think so.

"But," continues the objector, "this was faith and repentance toward *God*, and that was required by the law of Moses; but in the gospel we are required to have 'repentance toward God and faith in our Lord Jesus Christ,'" and the above words of Paul are cited as proof. Let us read the statement with its connections. Paul had invited the elders of Ephesus to visit him, and when they came, among other things he said to them:

"I kept back nothing that was profitable unto you, but have shewed you, and have taught you publicly, and from house to house, testifying both to the Jews, and also to the Greeks, repentance toward God, and faith toward our Lord Jesus Christ."—Acts 20: 20, 21.

This is the scriptural knife with its razor edge, with which so much hairsplitting is done in a vain attempt to prepare material from which to construct another way than that "cast up" by the Lord. Just how any people can have faith towards God from a christian standpoint of view, and not have faith in Christ, or *vice versa*, on which ever side of his earthly career they live, I confess I am not able to see. Let it be remembered that Paul, in both instances, was addressing those who professed faith in Christ, and it is reasonable to assume that to both Hebrews and Ephesians he preached the same things, the same word, the same gospel, and when he talked to the Hebrews in one place, of "faith toward God" and to Jews (Hebrews) and Greeks, in another place, of "faith toward our Lord Jesus Christ," evidently he was talking of one and the same thing. He certainly was not double minded nor double tongued. If so, he was not in a very excellent way just then. "The double minded man is unstable in all his ways," saith James, our Lord's brother.

Further: if this contention be allowed, then the doctrine of the resurrection and eternal judgment can not be regarded as part of the teaching of Christ. That he and his apostles taught both is too well known by Bible readers to need any proof here; and if those who make the objection we are considering, in order to have it appear that the observance of the ordinances of baptism in water for the remission of sins and the laying on of hands for the gift of the Holy Ghost, are unnecessary in our day, do not wish to give up the blessings which come by faith and repentance, and if they do not wish to lose the hope of the resurrection of the dead, and if they are not ready to give up the doctrine of eternal judgment, then they must withdraw this objection; for, if the objection is valid, and does away with baptism and the laying on of hands, it is equally valid in doing away with faith, repentance, resurrection and eternal judgment. Why not?

This argument, then, proves too much, and, as the old adage goes, proves nothing, only that those who make it do not know the more excellent way.

It will not take long to find out whether the principles of doctrine as referred to by Paul in the 6th chapter of Hebrews, belonged alone to the Mosaic dispensation, or whether they belonged also to the gospel as taught by Christ. If it can be shown that each of these principles of faith or doctrine were taught by *him*, the question will be settled in the minds of all except those referred to in chapter 1, who, unwittingly or otherwise, make the claim that the way of life as revealed in the gospel, as set forth in the New Testament, is not so excellent as some of the ways invented by men.

Did he teach faith as a part of the gospel law by which souls were made free from sin?

"Ye believe in God, *believe* also in *me.*"—John 14:1.

"For God so loved the world, that he gave his only begotten Son, that whosoever *believeth* in him should not perish, but have everlasting life."—John 3:16.

"Repent ye, and *believe* the gospel."—Mark 1:15.

Did he teach repentance?

"Except ye *repent*, ye shall all likewise perish."—Luke 13:3.

"Thus it is written, and thus it behoves Christ to suffer, and to rise from the dead the third day: and that *repentance* and remission of sins should be preached in his name among all nations" etc.,—Luke 24:46, 47.

"I came not to call the righteous but sinners to *repentance.*"

Did he teach the baptism of water as being efficacious in the salvation of sinners?

"He that believeth and is *baptized* shall be *saved.*"—Mark 16:16.

"Baptizing them in the name of the Father, and of the Son, and of the Holy Ghost."—Matt. 28:19.

"Verily, verily, I say unto thee, Except a man be *born* of water and of the Spirit, he can-*not* enter into the kingdom of God."—John 3:5.

Did he teach the resurrection of the dead—all the dead?

"And as touching the dead, *that they* rise: have ye not read in the book of Moses, how in the bush God spake unto him, say-ing, I am the God of Abraham, and the God of Isaac, and the God of Jacob?" etc.,—Mark 12:26.

"I am the resurrection, and the life: he that believeth in me, though he were dead, yet *shall he live.*"—John 11:25.

"Marvel not at this: for the hour is coming, in the which all that are in the graves shall hear his voice, and *shall come forth*; they that have done good, unto the resurrection of life; and they that have done evil, unto the resurrection of damnation."—John 5:28, 29.

Did Jesus teach the doctrine of "eternal judgment?"

"He that rejecteth me, and re-ceiveth not my words, hath one that judgeth him: the word that I have spoken, the same shall judge him *in the last day.*"—John 12:48.

"When the Son of man shall come in his glory, and all the holy angels with him, then shall he sit upon the throne of his glory: and before him shall be gathered all nations; and he shall separate them one from another, as a shepherd divideth his sheep from the goats," etc., etc.—Matt. 25:31, 32.

"As therefore the tares are gathered and burned in the fire; so shall it be in the end of this world. The Son of man shall send forth his angels, and they shall gather out of his kingdom all things that offend, and them which do iniquity; and shall cast them into a furnace of fire: there shall be wailing and gnashing of teeth. Then shall the righteous shine forth as the sun in the kingdom of their Father. Who hath ears to hear, let him hear."—Matt. 13: 40-43.

We are informed in the Scriptures that "in the mouth of two or three witnesses every word shall be established," and I have given *three* testimonies or evidences, from the "sayings" of Jesus while on earth which show that he did teach *five* of the six principles of doctrine referred to by Paul, years before the book of Hebrews was written. Then, reader, is it not an "established" fact that these five tenets of faith constituted just so much of the gospel plan of salvation, or "law of the Spirit of life in Christ Jesus," and are therfore "principles of the doctrine of Christ?" Yes, most assuredly.

Is it not an "established" fact that these five "principles of doctrine" constitute just so much of the law of the Lord, which is perfect and converts the soul? If you say "no," then I answer that Jesus spent a great deal of time in teaching what was not his doctrine, nor yet his Father's. Could he do that and yet be "the faithful and true witness?" (Rev. 1: 5).

If, as is claimed, faith is the only condition of salvation, or the only prerequisite essential to salvation, or in other words, if faith is the only point of doctrine that it is necessary for the sinner to accept in order to be saved, or to be converted, then when Jesus had established that *one* point of doctrine, he had taught *all* of the "law of the Lord," which is "perfect." To deny that proposition is to deny that faith only is sufficient to "convert" or save the soul. All those, then, who believe in the doctrine of salvation by faith *only* are bound by the logic of the above proposition.

Now, remember that it is the "law of the Lord" that converts the soul, and if faith in Christ is the only thing the sinner is required to have or do in order to be converted, saved, then when Christ had taught the principle of faith, he had taught *all* that was necessary to convert and save the soul, hence he had taught all the law of the Lord. It follows, then, that repentance baptism, resurrection and eternal judgment are not included in "the law of the Lord," or "perfect law of liberty," or "law of the Spirit of life;" for if they were they would convert, bless, or make the soul free from sin and death. (See Ps. 19: 7; Jas. 1: 25; Rom. 8: 2).

It further follows that repentance, baptism, resurrection and eternal judgment are not the principles of the doctrine of Christ, nor yet of his Father. Why, then, should *he* teach them? If they are not his doctrine, then whose are they? He found fault with the Pharisees for "teaching for doctrine the commandments of men." (Mark 7: 9). Did he do the same thing? No, a thousand times no.

"My doctrine is not mine but *his that sent me.*"—John 7: 16.

"For I have not spoken of myself: but the Father which sent me, he gave me a commandment, what I should say, and what I should speak."—John 12: 49.

Who, that believes these statements of Jesus, can believe he spent more time in teaching and explaining things that were not essential to salvation, than he did in teaching the one and only thing needful to convert and save the soul? Yet this is exactly what he did, if faith only, ·as is commonly taught, is that which converts or saves, to the exclusion of all other principles of doctrine as taught by Christ.

"But," says one, "you can find no three statements of Jesus in which is taught the laying on of hands for the gift of the Holy Ghost; you cannot, therefore, prove it to be one of the principles of his doctrine; why did you pass over it without notice? Was it not because you knew there was nothing in all the sayings of Jesus in favor of the laying on of hands for the gift of the Holy Ghost?"

Now, kind reader, I will be perfectly frank with you; I freely confess that I know of no statement in the New Testament accredited to Jesus while he was on earth, directly touching the laying on of hands for the reception of the Holy Ghost. Will you argue because of this fact, that it is not one of the principles of his doctrine? If so, then *if there were* such statements of his on record directly teaching it, it would certainly prove it to be one of the principles of his doctrine, wouldn't it?

"O yes," continues the objector, "it would prove it, but you can find no place where he mentions it, therefore you can*not* prove it."

Well, I have found where he taught repentance, baptism, resurrection, eternal judgment, and if your logic is good that proves that each of these *is* a principle of the doctrine of Christ. You must accept that proposition or reject your own logic. Which will you do?

Again: If a direct statement of Jesus Christ on the point of laying on of hands for the gift of the Holy Ghost would prove it to be a principle of his doctrine, then the same kind of a statement on any other point would also prove it to be his doctrine too. Listen.

"And these signs shall follow them that believe: *' * * *they shall lay hands on the sick* and they shall recover."—Mark 16: 17, 18.

Are my objecting friends willing to stand by the logic of their own position? If so they *must* accept the laying on of hands for the healing of the sick, and if they can do that they should not object to it for the gift of the Holy Ghost, and if they cannot, then, with them, a plain statement of Jesus is not regarded as proof; hence they are not willing to walk in the light of his teachings; they do not have confidence in him as being "*the* way," or as teaching "the more excellent way" to be saved.

I will here leave this point, however, for the present, and introduce another line of argument to show that Jesus *did* teach the doctrine of baptism for the remission of sins and also the laying on of hands for the gift of the Holy Ghost.

As before stated, the apostles were sent to preach the gospel of Christ as he instructed and commanded them. Christ sent them, as he was sent. He was sent with "a commandment what he should say and what he should speak." In addressing his Father in prayer he says:

"I have given unto them [the apostles—disciples] *the words which thou gavest me and they have received them.*"—John 17: 8.

Long before this God had promised:

"I will raise up unto them a Prophet like unto thee, and will put my words in his mouth; and he shall speak all the words that I shall command him."—Deut. 18: 18.

If God put his words into the mouth of Jesus and he again gave them to his apostles, "and they went forth and preached everywhere" in such an acceptable manner that the "Lord worked with them confirming the word with signs following," then who can be so obtuse as not to be able to see that they were teaching as he had commanded them? Or in other words, Who can fail to see that they taught the people just as he taught them? If then we can find that *they* taught baptism for the remission of sin and the laying on of hands for the gift of the Holy Ghost, who could ask for stronger proof that they were just so much of "the more excellent way" as taught by Christ himself?

As we have seen, those who were converted and added to the church on the day of Pentecost "continued steadfastly in the apostles' doctrine." Their doctrine was Christ's doctrine, for he had sent them to "preach the gospel to every creature," "to teach [it—the gospel, to] all nations," and these apostles to whom this commission was given stood there, and Matthias also stood with them in the place that had been made vacant by the fall of Judas, and Peter as mouth-piece or spokesman for the whole, in answer to the inquiry, "What shall we do," said: "Repent, and be baptized every one of you in the name of Jesus Christ, for the remission of sins, and ye shall receive the gift of the Holy Ghost."—Acts 2: 38.

This settles the question as to baptism being a part of the "apostles' doctrine." And when we consider that these men were filled with the Holy Ghost at the time the above statement was made and that they were acting under the authority of a high and holy calling and ordination to the apostolic office (and their ordinations all but one under the spotless hands of the Son of God himself) we cannot doubt that they were fully qualified to point out with certainty "the more excellent way."

Notice, too, that a promise was made that those who would repent and be baptized should, in some way, receive the gift of the Holy Ghost. The reception on the part of the repentant, baptized believer, of the Holy Ghost was included in the apostles' doctrine, and as such was evidently a part of "the more excellent way." In the 8th chapter of Acts we read:

"Then Philip went down to the city of Samaria, and preached *Christ* unto them. And the people with one accord gave heed unto those things which Philip spake, hearing and seeing the miracles which he did."—vs. 5, 6.

What did Philip preach? He preached *Christ*. What or who was Christ? He himself answers: "I am *the* way." Philip, then, preached "the way" in preaching Christ, or, in other words, he preached the way that Christ preached, that the apostles preached, for we must not forget that they all preached the same thing and that they all taught and walked in the old paths, and in so doing found rest to their souls.

We have seen that Peter on the day of Pentecost enjoined baptism as a part of the more excellent way to receive remission of sins and the gift of the Holy Ghost. Did Philip preach that same way? Let us see.

"But when they believed Philip preaching the things concerning *the kingdom of God, and the name of Jesus Christ*, they were baptized, both men and women."—v. 12.

Query: Why should they be baptized *when* they believed the preaching of the things concerning the kingdom of God?

Answer: Because, "Verily, verily, I say unto you, Except a man be *born* [baptized] *of water* and of the Spirit, he *cannot enter into the kingdom of God.*"—John 3: 5.

Thus had Jesus taught; thus had Philip believed; thus he taught the Samaritans as he preached Christ—the way—to them; and it is no wonder they were baptized after having been taught that they could not enter into the kingdom without it. Do any of my readers doubt that they were so taught? If so, then they doubt the statement that Philip preached "the things of the kingdom" or else they doubt that Jesus ever said what he is reported to have said to Nicodemus in John 3: 5, or what is probably still worse, they doubt the truthfulness of what he did say.

Query again: Why were these Samaritans baptized when they believed the things concerning the *name* of Jesus Christ.

Listen! "Go ye therefore and teach all nations, baptizing them *in the name* of the Father, and of the *Son* [Jesus Christ], and of the Holy Ghost."—Matt. 28: 19.

In preaching to them the things concerning the name of Jesus Christ Philip had told them of this command to the ministry of Jesus to baptize *in his name;* hence they were baptized *when* they believed it. Who would have done otherwise then? Who could do otherwise now? Who indeed?

He who announced himself to be "*the way*" had commanded his apostles to baptize the nations in his name; and this was tanta mount to a command to the nations to be baptized; and this command was doubtless based upon the principle that they could not enter into the kingdom of God without it; and these Samaritans, comprehending this fact, evidently regarded it as a more excellent way to enter the kingdom of God, hence they were baptized, both men and women, and had great joy; and I ask again, Who except those who do *not* believe "the things concerning the kingdom of God and the name of Jesus Christ" can ever do otherwise?

In the same chapter we find the account of the baptism by this same Philip of "A man of Ethiopia, an eunuch of great authority under Candace queen of the Ethiopians." He had been up to Jerusalem to worship and was returning to his home in his chariot and was reading from the book of "Esaias the prophet" when Philip saw him, and at the command of the Spirit went up close to the chariot and finally upon invitation of the eunuch took a seat with him in the chariot and "opened his mouth, and began at the same scripture [that the eunuch had been reading] and preached unto him Jesus." (verse 35). Preached what? Preached Jesus—*the way* —"the good way"—"the more excellent way." Evidently he preached to this man just as he had preached to the residents of Samaria—preached "the things concerning the kingdom of God"—how that it is impossible for a man to enter into it except he is baptized of water and of the Spirit; and how that the Savior had said salvation should come to those who believed and were baptized in his name; and hence it is no wonder that he, recognizing the importance of walking in "the way" which was preached to him, and understanding that Jesus whom Philip had just been preaching to him, had taught that entrance into the kingdom of God on the part of any man depended upon whether he was "born of water and of the Spirit" should be anxious to be baptized.

"And as they went on their way, they came unto a certain water: and the eunuch said, See, here is water; what doth hinder me to be baptized." (verse 36).

Why did he ask this question? Because Philip preached it to him as one of the things concerning the kingdom of God and the name of Jesus Christ; or, if he did not, then the eunuch did not believe the things of the kingdom, and if he did not believe them then he was not a proper subject for baptism; for "he that *believeth* and is baptized shall be saved." Philip could not do better than to preach the way to be saved; so this must have been "the more excellent way," and wo to him who "climbeth up some other way."

CHAPTER III.

The object of this writing is to show that the more excellent way to be saved is by the gospel of Christ in its fullness and perfection, and not to raise any one principle or part of that gospel to a higher importance than another. And though, so far, I have said much more on the two principles of baptism and laying on of hands than upon other points, faith, repentance, etc., it is not to make it appear that they are more important or more essential to salvation, but because fewer people see that they are of *equal* importance in making up "the more excellent way."

I do not wish to weaken the faith of any, nor do I desire to discourage any one in a genuine repentance, for these are so much of the way as "cast up" by the Lord, and cannot be dispensed with by those who would walk therein. But no more can baptism in water, and the laying on of hands, resurrection, eternal judgment, or any other part of the teachings of Christ be dispensed with by any one who would follow the Lord "whithersoever he goeth." (Matt. 8: 19). I trust this fact will be made plain to all in what has been, and is yet to be, presented, so that every one who has any desire to walk in the "good way" may do so, and in so doing find rest to their souls.

Returning again to the Samaritans we read:.

"Now when the apostles which were at Jerusalem heard that Samaria had received the word of God, they sent unto them Peter and John: who, when they were come down, prayed for them, that they might receive the Holy Ghost: (for as yet he was fallen upon none of them: only they were baptized in the name of the Lord Jesus). Then laid they their hands on them, and they received the Holy Ghost."—Acts 8: 14–17.

We have already seen how this same Peter, with this same John, and ten other men, all clothed with apostolic authority, stood up, and, under the inspiration of the Spirit of God, promised the people who were anxiously inquiring what to do, that they should receive the gift of the Holy Ghost on condition: "Repent, and be baptized every one of you in the name of Jesus Christ for the remission of sins." (Acts 2: 38).

The people at Jerusalem on the day of Pentecost, or some of them at least, gladly received the word and were baptized. We are not told how they received the Spirit, nor are we told that they did receive it; but it stands to reason that they would not have "continued steadfastly in the apostles' doctrine" if they had not. It is evident too, that these apostles taught and practiced alike at Jerusalem and Samaria, as well as all other places, and hence the doctrine called "the apostles' doctrine," and in which the Pentecostians are said to have "steadfastly continued," included the laying on of hands, with prayer for the gift of the Holy Ghost; and while there is no mention made of the laying on of hands at Jerusalem on Pentecost day, I think it is more excellent to believe they did, than to believe they were double minded, and preached and practiced one way at Jerusalem and another way at Samaria.

Why should the "apostles which were at Jerusalem" send Peter and John to the Samaritans when they heard that they had "received the word of God?"

Answer: Evidently because, "This is the word which by the gospel was preached unto them." It was a part of the apostles' doctrine. It was at Samaria, at any rate; why not at every other place? The "word of God" through his Son, was that a man cannot enter into the kingdom of God except through the birth of the water and of the Spirit. Philip, Peter and John all preached the word of God, or the things concerning the kingdom of God, which the Samaritans believed and received, and this preaching on the part of these ministers, and especially of Philip, and the belief and acceptation of what was preached on the part of the people at Samaria, led to their baptism and also to their confirmation by the laying on of hands. I presume that no one will dispute that fact.

If, then, the baptism and confirmation of these Samaritan converts resulted from the preaching of the things concerning the kingdom of God and the name of Jesus Christ, it is certain that baptism in water for the remission of sins, as also the laying on of hands for the gift of the Holy Ghost, was included in the apostles' doctrine, and if it was included in theirs it was in Christ's, and if it was included in His, it was in God's, for Jesus says, "My doctrine is not mine but his that sent me," and it is no wonder the converts at Jerusalem continued steadfastly in that doctrine.

It was Peter who said at Jerusalem, "Ye shall receive the gift of the Holy Ghost." It was Peter who was sent (with John) by the rest of the apostles at Jerusalem, to Samaria, that those whom Philip had baptized might receive the Holy Ghost. In both cases he was carrying out the commission he had received from Jesus Christ, to "preach the gospel to every creature" (Mark 16: 15), to "teach all nations baptizing them in the name of the Father, and of the Son, and of the Holy Ghost, teaching them to observe *all* things whatsoever I have *commanded you."* (Matt. 28: 19, 20).

Does the reader believe that Peter taught to observe more or less than Jesus commanded? If so, then you can have no faith in his ministrations, for it was upon condition that he and his brethren should teach the observance of such things as he commanded, that Jesus made the promise, "Lo! I am with you alway, even unto the end of the world." And Mark bears testimony to the acceptability of their teaching thus:

"And they went forth, and preached everywhere, the Lord working with them, and confirming the word with signs following."—Mark 16: 20.

This is proof of the strongest character, that the apostles preached as instructed and commanded by Jesus, unless we can believe the Lord worked with them and confirmed something which he had not commanded. Who would take the responsibility to charge the Lord with such work. Notice, too, that "they went forth and preached everywhere," in such manner that the Lord was pleased to confirm to those who received the word the truthfulness of the message the apostles bore to the world. Jerusalem and Samaria were included in what was contemplated in the "everywhere" where they preached and where the Lord worked with them; hence, at Jerusalem, and at Samaria, as also at other places—"everywhere"—they were evidently teaching the people to observe only what, and all of what Jesus had commanded. The Holy Ghost, too, which he had promised, came, as he told them it would, and by it "signs and great miracles" (Acts 8: 13, margin) were done in confirmation of the word preached. This fact, of itself, is proof sufficient to show that the Spirit that Jesus promised was received; and a part of its office work was:

"He shall teach you *all* things, and bring *all* things to your remembrance whatsoever I have said unto you."—John 14: 26.

If, then, Peter and John (with others) were filled with the Holy Ghost on the day of Pentecost, and if these men, together with Philip, were filled with it at Samaria—and evidently they were, or they could not have imparted it through their prayers and ministrations—and if the Holy Ghost performed its office work, as previously announced by Christ, then whatever they said or did under the inspiration of the Holy Ghost, was what Jesus himself had said to them, and told them to teach others—"all nations"—to observe; for the Spirit was to bring to their remembrance what he had said to them.

Therefore, when they preached the things concerning the kingdom of God, and the name of Jesus Christ, it was because they remembered that he had said these things unto them. When Peter said, "Repent every one of you and be baptized in the name of Jesus Christ," it was because he remembered that Jesus had said the same to him (and others); and when he added "for the remission of sins," it was because he remembered that Jesus had said, "He that believeth and is baptized shall be saved." And again: "Except a man be born [baptized] of water and of the Spirit he cannot enter into the kingdom of God." He remembered that his Lord had taught him that it was a saving ordinance, for elsewhere he says:

"The like figure whereunto even baptism doth also now save us (not the putting away of the filth of the flesh, but the answer of a good conscience toward God) by the resurrection of Jesus Christ."—1 Pet. 3: 21.

When Peter and John went to Samaria and laid their hands upon those whom Philip had baptized, they did it because, under the inspiration of the Spirit of truth, they remembered that among the principles of the doctrine of Christ was to be found the laying on of hands for the gift of the Holy Ghost. They must have remembered it as one of the "all things" Jesus had said they should teach the people to observe.

We must either believe this, or else we must believe that these men did that which they were not commanded to do, but that they did it upon their own authority; and that they acted, not under the direction of the Holy Ghost, which would cause them to remember "whatsoever" Jesus had said, but under the influence of a spirit that caused them to forget that they were sent out to represent Christ— the way—and not to set up their own ideas (Jewish or otherwise) instead, thus trying to "climb up some other way."

I cannot believe they would do that; and if any of my readers do, let them read the defense that Peter and John make for themselves, as if against this imputation:

"For we cannot but speak the things which we have seen and heard."—Acts 4: 20.

"Seen and heard!" From whom? From Jesus Christ, of course. How, then, can any one doubt that when they were teaching and practicing baptism and the laying on of hands, they were teaching and practic-

ing as Jesus had instructed, nay, had *commanded?*

"And it shall come to pass, that whosoever will not hearken unto my words which he [Christ] shall speak in my name, I will require it of him."—Deut. 18: 19.

Again:

"Him shall ye hear in all things whatsoever he shall say unto you, and * * * every soul which will *not* hear that prophet, shall be destroyed from among the people."—Acts 3: 22, 23.

To the apostles Jesus said on one occasion:

"He that heareth you heareth me."—Luke 10: 16.

And again:

"Verily, verily, I say unto you, He that receiveth whomsoever I send receiveth me; and he that receiveth me receiveth him that sent me."—John 13: 20.

Now in the light of these statements, who can for a moment doubt that any one who receives (obeys) the testimony of Jesus and of the apostles with reference to baptism for the remission of sins, or the laying on of hands for the gift of the Holy Ghost, or any other matter, will receive reward for so doing? On the other hand, those who do not receive, hear (obey) the same testimony "shall be destroyed from among the people."

Wherefore, dear reader,

"See that ye refuse not him that speaketh [whether by his own mouth or by the mouth of his servants]. For if they escaped not who refused him that spake on earth [Moses], much more shall not we escape, if we turn away from him that speaketh from heaven [Christ]:"—Heb. 12: 25; see also Heb. 2: 2, 3.

In the foregoing statements and others that might be given, two very important points are set forth clearly.

1. Baptism and the laying on of hands are both included in the principles of the doctrine taught by Christ and his apostles; that is, the words of teaching on these subjects and others, as quoted, were put into the mouth of Jesus by his Father, and he, in turn had given them to his apostles; and they had received them, and taught them to others, not as their own, but as the doctrine of Christ.

2. "Every soul" who hears his words on these as on all other subjects, is required to receive them, or to refuse to do so under penalty of being "destroyed from among the people."

The reader is now invited to carefully consider what is set forth in the following verses of Scripture.

"And a certain Jew named Apollos, born at Alexandria, an eloquent man, and mighty in the scriptures, came to Ephesus. This man was instructed in the way of the Lord; and being fervent in the spirit, he spake

and taught diligently the things of the Lord, knowing only the baptism of John. And he began to speak boldly in the synagogue: whom when Aquila and Priscilla had heard, they took him unto them, and expounded unto him the way of God more perfectly."
—Acts 18: 24-26.

The above quotation represents Apollos as, (1) an eloquent man, (2) mighty in the scriptures; (3) instructed in the way of the Lord; (4) fervent in spirit; (5) teaching diligently the things of the Lord: and those are certainly very praiseworthy qualifications in a minister; but it also represents him as "knowing only the baptism of John" or baptism in water as practiced by John.

In Mark 1:4, 5 we read:

"John did baptize in the wilderness, and preach the baptism of repentance for the remission of sins. And there went out unto him all the land of Judea, and they of Jerusalem, and were all baptized of him in the river of Jordan, confessing their sins." (See also Matt. 13:1, 5, 6).

Three important points are set forth in the foregoing: 1, In John's message was the doctrine of repentance and baptism. 2, He baptized those who came to him, giving evidence of their repentance. 3, *Both* repentance and baptism were "for the remission of sins."

Now, Apollos knew all this; but it seems he did not know the baptism of the Holy Ghost through the laying on of hands; but at the same time he was "instructed in the way of the Lord" so far as he had gone. Moreover, "he spake and taught diligently the things of the Lord."

Now, if Apollos knew *only* the baptism of John, and at the same time was "instructed in the way of the Lord," how can we escape the conclusion that the baptism of John was the way of the Lord? And if it is the way of the Lord, is there "a more excellent way?" I think not.

Again: If Apollos knew only the baptism of John, or baptism in water, preceded by repentance, based upon proper faith in the Messiah, and all for the remission of sins, as we have seen John taught—if he knew only these things, and yet "taught diligently the things of the Lord," how shall we escape the conclusion that baptism is one of the "things" which the Lord requires of the penitent believer "for the remission of sins."

But up to this time Apollos had not learned all the way of the Lord, and so Aquila and Priscilla took him into their house and gave him a more perfect understanding of "the way of God;" "expounded unto him the way of God more perfectly," says the record.

In the way of God, then, there

was something besides baptism in water, or "the baptism of John;" something besides repentance, something besides abstract faith; something without which "the way of the Lord" as taught by Apollos was not complete.

The following will explain more fully the way of God.

"And it came to pass that while Apollos was at Corinth, Paul having passed through the upper coasts came to Ephesus: and finding certain disciples, he said unto them, Have ye received the Holy Ghost since ye believed? And they said unto him, We have not so much as heard whether there be any Holy Ghost. And he said unto them, Unto what then were ye baptized? And they said, Unto John's baptism. Then said Paul, John verily baptized with the baptism of repentance, saying unto the people, that they should believe on him which should come after him, that is, on Christ Jesus. When they heard this, they were baptized in the name of the Lord Jesus. And when Paul had laid his hands upon them, the Holy Ghost came on them; and they spake with tongues, and prophesied."— Acts 19: 1–6.

Perhaps these people had been baptized by Apollos before Aquila and Priscilla had taught him the way of God more perfectly, while he yet knew only the baptism of John. Perhaps they had been baptized by some one who didn't know even as much as Apollos; at any rate, they had not received the Holy Ghost, nor had they, according to their own statement, heard there was such a thing; they had, however, heard of John's baptism in water, and had received it, or thought they had at least; but Paul's reasoning seems to have convinced them that there was some mistake. He says: "John verily baptized with the baptism of repentance, saying unto the people, that they should believe on him [Christ] that should come after him," and baptize them "with the Holy Ghost." (See also Mark 1: 8). That is to say, John baptized such as brought "forth fruits meet for repentance," and did it "for the remission of sins," and told the people that Christ would baptize them with the Holy Ghost, and I believe he told them that the Holy Ghost should be given through the laying on of hands.

But there is no reference made in any of the statements attributed to John, in the New Testament, that even mentions the laying on of hands, says one. Well, what of it? If that proves that he did not understand and teach the laying on of hands, then the fact that no mention is made by him of the resurrection or of eternal judgment proves that he did not understand and teach them. Again, there is no place in the New Testament where mention is made of any assertion by John that faith is necessary to salvation. At least the writer knows of none. Shall I say because of this, that John did not believe that faith is necessary to salvation? Surely not.

But whether John did or did not teach the laying on of hands, Paul evidently did; and when the disciples, whom he found at Ephesus, received additional light from his instructions, and were baptized, he laid his hands on them and as a result the Holy Ghost came upon them, thus showing that God approved what was done and said.

Why were they so ready to receive the laying on of hands, if Paul had not taught them in regard to it? Evidently Paul was as able to "expound the way of God' perfectly, as was Aquila and Priscilla, and it seems they were able to instruct one who was "mighty in the Scriptures" and "fervent in the Spirit," and who was already "instructed in the way of the Lord," but not perfectly, because he knew only the baptism of John; and Paul was able to instruct those who had, as they thought, received the baptism of John, and didn't know any more, having never heard of the Holy Ghost, through the laying on of hands, or otherwise.

Presuming, and I think no one will say that it is not a fair presumption, that Paul taught those disciples at Ephesus "the way of God more perfectly," just as Aquila and Priscilla taught it to Apollos, and who can doubt that "the way of God" as more perfectly taught has in it the laying on of hands for the gift of the Holy Ghost? And, if that is God's way, who can doubt that it is the more excellent way to receive the Holy Ghost?

"But," continues the objector, "you forget that Cornelius and his household all received the Holy Ghost without baptism or the laying on of hands." No, reader, I do not forget it. I remember to have read it time and time again, and I have not only not forgotten it, but I hope I never shall.

"But what are you going to do with him then?"

Nothing at all. He has passed over to the other side, and entered into his reward and I could not do anything with him if I would. But if I could meet a man just like Cornelius was, I should be much pleased to take him into the church in the same way Peter did Cornelius and his household, and that is more than any objector with whom I have ever talked, would agree to do.

Let it be remembered that the Apostle Peter who ministered for Cornelius and his house, was the same Peter who, about seven or eight years before, had stood up with his fellow apostles, and told that vast concourse of people at Jerusalem to "repent and be baptized," and promised them that they should "receive the gift of the Holy Ghost." Do you think the gospel order has changed during these years? Certainly not. Has Peter found out he was wrong on Pentecost day and changed his faith and ministrations? I think not. Well, what is the trouble; there seems to be a change somewhere, for in the one case the Holy Ghost was promised on condition that the people repent and be baptized, and in the other the Holy Ghost is received before baptism is even mentioned.

Cornelius was a gentile, and did not have the privilege of hearing and obeying the gospel as yet, and hence, as one who had no law, was doing, as best he could, "the things contained in the law," and showing "the works of the law written in his heart." (See Rom. 2: 14, 15). Of him the record says:

"A devout man, and one that feared God with all his house, and gave much alms to the people and *prayed to God alway.* He saw in a vision evidently about the ninth hour of the day an angel of God coming in to him, and saying unto him, Cornelius. And when he looked on him, he was afraid, and said, What is it, Lord? And he said unto him, Thy prayers and thine alms are come up for a memorial before God. And now send men to Joppa, and call for one Simon, whose surname is Peter: he lodgeth with one Simon, a tanner, whose house is by the seaside: he shall tell thee what thou oughtest to do."—Acts 10: 2-6.

Cornelius sent for Peter as directed, and Peter, having his prejudice against the gentiles removed by a vision, and the voice of the Spirit, went as requested, and took six of his brethren with him; and after making apology for entering in the house of a gentile, said: "I ask therefore for what intent ye have sent for me." (v. 29).

The next three verses tell in Cornelius' own words how he was directed to send for Peter, and the 33d verse says:

"Immediately therefore I sent to thee; and thou hast well done that thou art come. Now therefore are we all here present before God, to hear all things that are *commanded* thee of God."

Verses 34 to 43 tell, in Peter's own words, of his perception that God is no respecter of persons, of "how God anointed Jesus of Nazareth with the Holy Ghost and with power;" of his crucifixion, of his resurrection, of his being shown openly to chosen witnesses, of his ordination "to be the judge of quick and dead," and of the fact that:

"To him give all the prophets witness, that through his name, whosoever believeth in him shall receive remission of sins. While Peter yet spake these words, the Holy Ghost fell on all them which heard the word. And they of the circumcision which believed were astonished, as many as came with Peter, because that on the Gentiles also was poured out the gift of the Holy Ghost. For they heard them speak with tongues, and magnify God. Then answered Peter, Can any man forbid water that these should not be baptized, which have received the Holy Ghost as well as we? And he *commanded* them to be baptized in the name of the Lord. Then prayed they him to tarry certain days.''—Verses 44–48.

I have been thus particular in presenting this matter to show, (1) that there is nothing in the case, when considered in all its bearings, to justify any one in using it as against baptism or the laying on of hands; and (2) to show that, as has been said before, not one who offers this objection, is willing to stand by the logic of the facts in the case.

Cornelius was a devout, praying, God-fearing man; not an ordinary sinner. So devout, and so humble had he become, that he received a visit from an angel, who gave him instruction as to what he should do to be saved, as witness the following: ''Send men to Joppa and call for Simon whose surname is Peter;

who shall, tell thee *words whereby thou and all thy house shall be saved.*''—Acts 11: 13, 14.

Wonderful privilege was Peter's to tell these precious souls what to do to be saved. Wonderful responsibility is his. He must not fail. The consequences are too awful. The happiness of immortal souls depends upon his faithfulness. They are ''ready to hear all things which are commanded him of God.'' Surely he will be faithful and tell them just what, and only what, he has been ''commanded of God.'' The only *command* that Peter gave them so far as the record states, is that in the 48th verse: ''And he commanded them to be baptized.''

''Ah! but the words by which they were to be saved are found in verse 43, where it says 'whosoever believeth on him shall receive remission of sins,''' says one.

But do you know that these were *all* of his words to which they were required to give heed? I have no objection to the words in verse 43; I rejoice in the thought contained therein. But I also believe the words in verse ·48. I believe that they, together with those in verse 43, and all others that Peter spake unto Cornelius on that occasion, were the ''words *whereby* thou and all thy house shall be saved,'' and as such were necessary to the salvation of that household; as the words spoken on the day of Pentecost by this same apostle, and sanctioned by his brethren of the same high and holy calling, and also by the Holy Ghost with which they were filled, were necessary to the salvation of the three thousand who gladly received the word on that day.

"But was not Cornelius already saved?" do you ask?

Let the angel that appeared to and talked with him answer.

"He shall tell thee words whereby thou and all thy house SHALL BE saved."

If he were already saved, then what need for Peter to be sent for, to tell him words whereby he *might be* saved? Echo answers "what need?" and no man can give a better answer.

But what words of Peter, on that occasion, were clothed with the power to save? Not those in verse 43 alone, nor those in verse 48 alone, nor yet in both of them. The key is found in verse 44.

"While Peter yet spake these words, the Holy Ghost came on all them which heard *the word.*"

What word?

"And this is *the word* which by *the gospel* is preached unto you." —1 Peter 1: 25.

Harmonious word! always the same.

Again:

"I am not ashamed of the gospel of Christ: for it is the power of God unto salvation to everyone that believeth; to the Jew first, and also to the Greek." —Rom. 1: 16.

Now, if the gospel is the power of God unto salvation and Peter was to tell Cornelius words whereby he should be saved, then he was to tell him the story of the gospel. From that logical conclusion there is no escape. That story, as we have seen, is not complete until "all things whatsoever he saith unto you" has been told. Until Cornelius and his friends had heard and observed "all things" that Jesus had commanded Peter and the rest of the apostles to teach, they had not heard and obeyed the word which by the gospel Peter preached unto them and which was the power of God unto their salvation.

A part of the gospel as taught by Christ was baptism in water for the remission of sins, as we have already seen, hence Peter "commanded them to be baptized." So even in the case of Cornelius this ordinance was a part of the more excellent way to be saved. IT IS SO IN EVERY CASE.

But how many professed christians of today will accept this case as a proper rule by which sinners are to be converted and received into the church? Not one who uses it as an argument against baptism or the laying on of hands have I ever seen who would, as a minister, receive such a one as Cornelius into his church or as a lay member would be willing to have him received.

In the fall of 1896 I met and conversed with a Rev. Mr. ——— in the state of Florida. During the conversation the question of baptism came up and at about the usual place the regulation question, "What will you do with Cornelius?" was asked by him.

I replied: "I will take all the 'men you can find like Cornelius into the church just like Peter took him in, but you wouldn't do it."

"Do you think not?" he asked, as if in surprise.

After assuring him that I meant what I said, I asked:

"Now if I should send men to you and tell you that I had seen an angel, and that the angel had told me to send for you and that you would tell me words whereby I should be saved, would you come and receive me into the church as Peter did him?"

"No sir," said he, "I don't believe in any such foolishness as that."

I think these were his exact words. He was a man with a collegiate education and was well equipped so far as that part is concerned, for preaching; and yet, everything connected with Cornelius' history as set forth in the 10th chapter of Acts, except the fact that he received the Holy Ghost *before* baptism, and "whosoever believeth in him shall receive remission of sins," is by him brushed to one side as is trash before the broom of the housewife and bluntly called "foolishness." I do not think that is the more excellent way.

But who could do any better while walking "in a way not cast up" by the *Lord* and prefers to walk in "a way that seemeth right unto a man" even though "the end thereof are the ways of death." (Prov. 14: 12).

No such man as Cornelius could secure a membership in any of the popular churches of today in the same way and with the same experience that he did then. His claim that he had been visited by an angel would be enough to cause his rejection by any minister; and any church who would reject baptism or laying on of hands because Cornelius received the Holy Ghost before he had received either of these ordinances; and every minister and every layman, and every church that refuses to believe in the efficacy of baptism and the necessity of laying on of hands, would prefer charges against any of their brethren and cast them out as heretics, if they should "magnify God" by speaking in tongues as did Cornelius and his company.

At the same time they claim to be converted just as Cornelius was and to the same faith in every particular, and seek to fortify themselves in such claim by the experience of Cornelius and his friends. They profess to believe that this little company of disciples were saved because of their faith in God and in Christ the Lord. They also believe they will themselves be saved by their faith in God and Christ. They believe that some day they will be permitted to enter into the presence of God and there meet Cornelius and join with him in singing praises to God and the Lamb; and yet his *faith* and experience was so much different from their own, that if he could appear among them today as he appeared in that little company in his own house in Cæsarea years ago, they would cast him out of their company and at once pronounce him a heretic. Can this be "the more excellent way."

The record does not inform us as to whether they received the laying on of hands for the gift of the Holy Ghost or not, nor does it state as a fact that they were baptized. But I think it very reasonable to believe that they received both.

Why should they after they had received the Holy Spirit, do you ask? The answer is easy enough. Baptism is not only for, or in order to, remission of sins, but it is also for the retaining of remission or forgiveness of sins once pardoned.

Even if we admit (a thing which cannot be proved) that all the sins of each individual in this company or of any of them were remitted, blotted out, and that before baptism, is it not reasonable to believe that those same sins or others, and perhaps both, would have come back on them if they had refused to heed Peter's command to them to be baptized? and especially so as he was to tell them what was commanded him of God? So the necessity of baptism is clearly seen even in this case.

And, though they received the Holy Ghost before the laying on of hands, yet as Peter had practiced this rite at Samaria and as it is one of the principles of the doctrine of Christ, if they had refused to accept it they doubtless would have lost the precious gift that God had graciously bestowed on them for a special purpose, as any one who will read the history of the case with honest purpose can see; and hence we see that even in their case the rite of laying on of hands was necessary, as otherwise how could they have retained what they had received, viz., the gift of the Holy Ghost.

I think it is a more excellent way to accept the doctrine of Christ as a whole than to accept only such parts as may suit our own notions; and hence I still believe in baptism and the laying on of hands, notwithstanding what is written concerning the reception of the Holy Ghost by Cornelius and his friends; for, as we have seen, there is nothing in it to prove that either ordinance is not necessary or essential to the purpose for which God ordained it; the one "for the remission of sins," the other "for the gift of the Holy Ghost."

To believe that Peter taught one way at one time and place, and another and different way at another time and place, is to believe that he was not inspired with the Holy Ghost; not "endued with power from on high;" but that he was double-minded, double-tongued and "unstable in all his ways." I cannot do that, and hence I believe that at Cæsarea, at Jerusalem, at Samaria, "everywhere" he preached and practiced alike and that God approved of his labors. And as he taught baptism in connection with remission of sins and the reception of the Holy Ghost at Jerusalem (Acts 2:38); and as he practiced laying on of hands with prayer for the gift of the Spirit at Samaria (Acts 8:17); and as he commanded baptism at Cæsarea (Acts 10:48), it is easy for the unprejudiced to see that in all these places he was teaching the principles of "the more excellent way."

CHAPTER IV.

I notice here one more objection made by those who do not believe in the saving efficacy of baptism, and then pass on to another line of thought.

It is claimed that the words of Jesus (John 3: 5), "born of water" do not mean baptism in water. The writer once held a discussion with a minister who made some pretentions to being a man of learning, and though he would not say what the words, "born of water," did mean, he claimed that they did not mean baptism, and said the idea of baptism was not in the meaning of the word "born" or its original. That the words are figurative, there can be no doubt, and that a real birth in the sense in which the word is ordinarily used, was not meant, is equally certain. What could be the reality of which "born of water" was the figure? Or what idea did Jesus wish to convey when he said, "Except a man be born of water and of the Spirit he cannot enter into the kingdom of God?" I offer the following as the concensus of opinion of the scholars of the world on this subject:

"But does born of water certainly mean baptism? Dr. J. R. Graves, Bro. Moody's senior editor, says: 'born of water' refers to the baptism of one previously born of the Spirit," and then adds: "It means nothing else and no Baptist that we ever heard or ever read of, ever believed otherwise, until A. Campbell frightened them away from an interpretation that is sustained by the concensus of opinion of all scholars of all denominations in all ages." I have quoted Dr. Graves to establish the one point that "born of water means baptism." — Nashville Debate, page 142. The debate was between Rev. Moody, Baptist, and Rev. Harding, Christian —Campbellite—and the quotation is from one of Mr. Harding's speeches.

Allowing that Dr. Graves was correct in the above statement, and the fact is established that "born of water means baptism," otherwise, nothing relating to the meaning of words can be established by human testimony. And if, by the words, "born of water," Jesus meant baptism in water, then no one who refuses to be baptized, when the opportunity is afforded him, can hope to enter into the kingdom of God.

From "The History of Sprinkling," by L. C. Wilson, Oskaloosa, Iowa, I quote as follows:

"Timothy Dwight, the greatest Rabbi of Presbyterians the New World has produced, says, Vol. 4, pp. 300, 301: '*To be born again* is precisely the same thing as to be born of water and the Spirit.' 'To be born of water is to be baptized.' 'He who, understanding the nature and authority of this institution, refuses to be baptized, WILL NEVER ENTER IN-TO THE VISIBLE NOR INVISIBLE KINGDOM OF GOD.' So affirms the president of Yale."—p. 132.

Again: Dr. Whitby, a scholarly Presbyterian, in commenting on John 3: 5, says:

"That our Lord here speaks of baptismal regeneration *the whole Christian church* from its *earliest times* has invariably taught."—History of Sprinkling, p. 133.

, Thus it is seen that Dr. Graves (Baptist) and Dr. Whitby (Presbyterian) agree in their testimony that the opinion of scholars in the various denominations, "in all ages" of the christian church, "from its earliest times," was that the words, "born of water," in John 3:5, refer to baptism. At least this was their opinion until, "A. Campbell frightened them away from" it. Dr. Dwight adds his illustrious name to the list, and emphasizes his opinion by saying, "He who, understanding the nature and authority of this institution, refuses to be baptized, will never enter into the visible nor invisible kingdom of God."

More testimony on this point it would seem would be superfluous, but some people have to be literally overwhelmed, submerged, covered, *baptized* with proofs in order to convert them to the scriptural idea of baptism, so I give the following from Dr. Wall, an Episcopalian:

"There is not any one writer of any antiquity in any language, but who understands it (John 3:5: 'Except a man be born of water and the Spirit he cannot enter into the kingdom of God') of baptism; and if it be not so understood, it is difficult to give an account how a person is born of water any more than born of wood."—History Infant Baptism, Vol. 1, p. 147; Scriptural Baptism pp. 120, 121.

Here I let the argument on this point rest with the remark that, as a Baptist, Dr. Graves did not believe in baptism as essential to salvation, nor did Dr. Dwight nor Dr. Whitby, as Presbyterians; but they evidently made honest statements of truth touching the point under consideration, notwithstanding the fact that their testimonies militated and still militates against their respective creeds. And while, under such circumstances, their testimony might have more weight than if they testified in favor of their own creeds, we see no good reason for rejecting the testimony of Dr. Wall, who, as an Episcopalian, may have believed in the saving efficacy of the ordinance of baptism, since they all substantially agree.

If the testimony of Drs. Graves, Dwight and Whitby be true, *their* creeds are utterly at fault as to the question of baptism, *i. e.* its saving efficacy, and if human testimony can establish a point at all, then it is established that "born of water," as used in John 3: 5, means baptism in water, and the whole question regarding the saving efficacy of that Holy Rite is settled in the mind of every person who believes in the divinity of Jesus, the Christ, and who *believes the statement* attributed to him in the third chapter of John. Who, then, "can forbid that" all who truly believe and repent should be baptized "for the remission of sins," as, without it, none can enter into the "visible nor invisible kingdom of God." Who will take upon himself the responsibility to cast out the sacred and holy ordinance and refuse to give it a place in the more excellent way to be saved.

Now, since the importance, yea, the necessity of baptism, is so clearly set forth, let us inquire what it is to be baptized. How is it to be performed?

Upon this question there are differences of opinion again. One class says, "By immersion only;" another, "By effusion only;" and still another, wishing to appear more liberal minded, and perhaps, to please all and avoid controversy, "by either of these methods, as best suits the fancy or convenience of the recipient of the ordinance, "just as though God was dependent upon the taste or caprice of mortal man to point out the method of keeping the solemn ordinance, without which, as we have seen, it is impossible for him to enter into the kingdom of God.

Has God no will in this matter? Has that will not been expressed? If he has a will and has not expressed it, is he not at fault? Would it not be strange if he should not express his will as to the *how*, when so much, yea, entrance into his kingdom, depends upon the doing of what is conveyed in the word baptism?

There are three ways by which men profess to obey this holy ordinance, but which is the more excellent way? Which is the way "cast up" by the Lord? Listen:

"Then cometh *Jesus* from Galilee to Jordan unto John, to be baptized of him."—Matt. 3:13.

Does Jesus know the way to be baptized? Will he walk in that way? Yea, verily. Now read:

"And Jesus, when he was baptized, went up straightway *out of the water*: and lo, the heavens were opened unto him, and he saw the Spirit of God descending like a dove, and lighting upon him: and lo a voice from heaven, saying, This is my beloved Son, in whom I am well pleased."—Verses 16, 17.

If, *when* Jesus was baptized, he went up straightway out of the water, does it not follow that just *before* he was baptized he went down into the water? Nothing can be clearer than that. So if Jesus knew the way and walked therein, in his example we have the proof that the more excellent way to be baptized is to go down into the water and come up straightway out of the water. Remember that he is "the way," and this way of baptism pleased not only himself but his Father as well; and the Father manifested his pleasure by permitting his own voice to be heard from heaven, saying, "This is my beloved Son in whom I am well pleased." Would the Father be so well pleased with any other than the more excellent way? So the more excellent way to be baptized, as attested by the example of Jesus and also by the voice of his Father, was by immersion in water, or going down into the water and coming up out of the water as did the Savior.

But did John baptize all others in that way?

"And there went out unto him [John] all the land of Judea, and they of Jerusalem, and were *all* baptized of him *in the river* of Jordan, confessing their sins."—Mark 1: 5.

Jesus went to Jordan unto John to be baptized, and was baptized by going down into the water and coming up out of it again. The people of Judæa and Jerusalem went to the same John and were baptized in the river of Jordan. Can it be possible for any one to read these two accounts and have any doubt as to the manner of baptism in either case? John was a man sent from God (John 1: 6), and as such certainly understood what would be pleasing to him, and so baptized by taking his candidates down into the water and baptizing them *in* the river of Jordan.

Philip understood the matter just as did John; for when he had preached Jesus unto the Ethiopian eunuch, and the eunuch demanded to know why he could not be baptized, and being informed that he could on condition, "If thou believest with all thine heart; "he commanded the chariot to stand still: and they went down both into the water, both Philip and the eunuch; and he baptized him. And when they were come up out of the water, the Spirit of the Lord caught away Philip, that the eunuch saw him no more: and he went on his way rejoicing."—Acts 8: 38, 39.

Here it is easy to see that Philip baptized in the same way

that John did, and that God sanctioned the work, else his Spirit would not have been present in such power that it caught away Philip that the eunuch saw him no more.   In the mind of Philip and the eunuch also, it was necessary to go down into the water in order that the eunuch might receive baptism. Have any of my readers a more excellent way?   A way that merits and receives the sanction and blessing of God is surely good enough, anyway.   In the foregoing cases of baptism but *one* method is pointed out, and that is immersion in water and coming again straightway up out of the water.   Sprinkling and pouring are entirely out of the question.   Again:

"And John also was baptizing in Ænon near to Salem because there was much water there: and they came and were baptized."—John 3:23.

If John had wished to sprinkle the people in the modern sense of that term, he would not have had any need for "much water." A very little would have sufficed to baptize all the people in Ænon, if a few drops of water sprinkled on the forehead was baptism. But John's way of baptizing required *much* water, and this element was to be found in great abundance at Ænon, hence the man sent of God (John 1:6) to baptize with water, repaired to that place to baptize

because there was much water there.   The only method of baptism in which a large quantity of water would be necessary is immersion, hence John must have immersed the people; and he being sent of God to do such work, as is shown above, it follows that he must have baptized in the more excellent way.

"But," says the objector, "it was not that much water was needed in which to baptize the people, but for culinary purposes, and for the multitudes to drink, and also for their horses."

Mr. A. C. Rogers, a Pedobaptist writer, says:

"Again (John 3:25), we read that while Christ was baptizing in Judea, and John was baptizing in Enon, near to Salem (because there was much water there—'Polla Hudata,' many springs, or watering places for drinking and culinary purposes necessary to the multitudes)," etc.—Christian Baptism, p. 16.

But how did Mr. Rogers, or any one else, find out that it was for drinking and culinary purposes that much water was needed? Not from the Bible, for it does not hint such a thing.   On the other hand it expressly declares that the reason why John *baptized* at Ænon was because there was much water there.

Not long since the writer visited one of the largest (if not the largest) electric plants in the world.   It was keeping in motion the street cars of the little city in which it is located, and those of a larger one twenty miles and more away, as well as sending cars back and forth between the two cities at regular intervals of only a few minutes. The machinery that generates the electricity which runs all these cars, is all run by water. The plant is situated on the banks of the famous Niagara River, and convenient to the rapids.

Why did the designers and builders of the plant select such a place for its location? "Because there was much water there." Why should they want much water? Was it because they expected to have great crowds come to see the wonderful machinery, and they wanted to furnish them water to drink, and for culinary purposes? Nonsense, do you say? Not any worse than to say that such was the reason that John baptized at Ænon. There was much water at Niagara, therefore the great electric plant, whose intricate machinery was to be moved by water, was placed there. That proposition will not be disputed by any one, I am sure. Nor would it be disputed if I should transpose it and say the plant was located at Niagara because there was much water there. No one would ever dream the much water was for "drinking or culinary purposes," but all would understand that much

water was needed to move the machinery and operate the plant.

There was much water in Ænon and therefore John went there to baptize, not to give the people a drink of water or a chance to wash their hands or to cook a meal of victuals. To say anything else is to dispute the Bible, for its language is clear, "John also was baptizing in Ænon near to Salem because there was much water there."

On this passage Richard Fuller says: "The Greek for 'much water' is *polla hudata*,' and the Pedobaptist translators have correctly rendered it 'much water.' But it is now pretended that the phrase only means 'many streams!' Again I ask, must there not be some mutiny of conscience? First, *hudor* never means 'stream.' It always means 'water.' The plural *hudata*, means 'waters,' and, of itself, imparts quantity."– Scriptural Baptism, page 76.

And on page 77 he quotes Doddridge thus:

"Nothing surely can be more evident than that *polla hudata*, 'many waters,' signifies a large quantity of water, it being sometimes used for the Euphrates." —Jer. 51: 13, (Septuagint).

And from Olshausen (vol. 2, p. 101) thus:

"John baptized at Ænon, because there was deep water there, convenient for immersion."

And again from Kuinol, vol. 3, p. 248:

"An abundance of water, so that the human body could be easily immersed in it, according to the mode of baptism as then practiced; *hudata* does not signify many streams, but an abundance of water as in Revelation 1: 15, and other places."—Ibid p. 78.

These three authors, Mr. Fuller claims, were Pedobaptist writers, and yet they agree with him, that the Greek words from which the English "much water" comes in the common version, signify "a large quantity of water," "convenient for immersion," "that the human body could be easily immersed in it." We all know that the English of it means the same thing, and so we have a strong presumptive proof in favor of immersion as the more excellent way, yea, the only way to be baptized.

Now, let us examine the meaning of the word baptize. When Jesus Christ commanded his apostles to baptize the nations, he certainly used a word, the meaning of which they fully understood. They could not have been ignorant of its import, or neither they nor the people were under any obligation to obey. To say that there was, or is, anything in the great commission which cannot be easily understood is a reflection against

Christ. None can afford to do that. That the pure Greek for baptize is *baptizo*, and for baptized is *baptistheis*, I believe there is no variation of opinion among scholars.

"The question before us, then, is this, what does *baptizo* mean? I answer it means immerse. It no more means to pour or sprinkle than it means to fly. * * * But in Greek *baptizo* means immerse. Our opponents have been, over and over, defied to produce a single instance where it means sprinkle or pour. They have ransacked all the Greek writings, and have failed."—Richard Fuller, Scriptural Baptism, page 16.

Some, perhaps, will say: Fuller was a Baptist, an immersionist, we cannot accept his testimony. Well, here are statements from those who are not Baptists, but believers in sprinkling or pouring, and yet candor seems to have compelled them to testify against themselves and their creeds:

Calvin.—"The word *baptizo* signifies to immerse, and the rite of immersion was performed by the ancient church."

Luther.—"Baptism is a Greek word, and may be translated immersion, as when we immerse anything in water that it may be wholly covered."

Beza.—"Christ commanded us to be baptized: by which word it is certain immersion is meant.

* * * To be baptized in water signifies no other than to be immersed in water, which is the external ceremony of baptism.''—Scriptural Baptism, p. 23.

Vitringa.—"The act of baptizing is the immersion of believers in water. Thus also it was performed by Christ and the apostles."

Gurtlerus. — "To baptize among the Greeks, is undoubtedly to immerse, to dip, and baptism is immersion, dipping."

Salmasius.—"Baptism is immersion, and was administered in former times, according to the force and meaning of the word."

The author of the Free Inquiry Respecting Baptism, Leipsic, 1802: "Baptism is perfectly identical with our word immersion or submersion. If immersion under water is for cleansing or washing, then the word means cleansing or washing."—p. 7. "The baptism of John and that of the apostles were performed in precisely the same way, that is, the candidate was completely immersed under water."—p. 36.

Bretschneider. — "An entire immersion belongs to the nature of baptism. This is the meaning of the word."

Scholy, on Matt. 3, 6: "Baptism consists in the immersion of the whole body in water.'—Scriptural Baptism, pp. 24–26.

These are selected from a large number of authors of great learning and it is believed that the testimony of these men, when united with the testimony of those favorable to immersion, and the plain statements of the English Scriptures, concerning the different baptisms of the New Testament, where we are told that people were baptized "*in* the river of Jordan," in a place where there was "much water," that "they went down into the water," and came "up straightway out of the water," in the performance of the act of baptism will be enough to convince even the most skeptical, provided they have honesty of heart and a desire for truth, that the meaning of the word *baptizo*, or baptize, is immersion and nothing else. And if that is the meaning of the word in Greek, the language in which the New Testament was written, it is certainly very clear that when Jesus said, "He that believeth and is baptized shall be saved," and, "Baptizing them," etc., he had in his mind, and conveyed to the mind of his apostles, the idea of immersion only, and that, to use Prof. Anthon's words to Dr. Parmly, "Sprinkling, etc., are entirely out of the question."—See Scriptural Baptism, p. 62.

But now comes Mr. A. F. Rogers in full war-paint dress, and being duly aroused and enthused, deposeth as follows:

"Whatever may have been the meaning of *baptidzo* in classic Greek, that has no bearing whatever on its meaning in the Bible; and to go to *this* source for its meaning *there*, is an insult to all intelligence, both human and divine, for this reason: Two hundred and eighty-five years before John the Baptist was born, the old Hebrew Scriptures were translated into Greek; and in this translation there were two Hebrew words, *"Rahats"* and *"Tabal,"* that must be rendered into Greek, and they both signified the same thing, WASHING or PURIFICATION. With this difference: *Rahats* signified any washing in things of common life, while *Tabal* was never used in this sense at all, but to express only purification from sin. It was a religious ordinance only, hence, these translators find *Lono* in Greek exactly answering to *Rahats* in Hebrew, and they substituted the one for the other; but when they look into the Greek for a word answering to *Tabal*, it is not there! Why? Because the Greeks were heathens, and had no use for a word that expressed only a religious ordinance of purification from sin. Now, there was but one thing they could do, and that was what they did: they substituted *Baptidzo* for *Tabal*, not because they were synonymous, but because it had some resemblance to the one they wanted. It's

original among the Greeks, therefore, has nothing whatever to do with its Bible meaning; since it has been made a substitute for *Tabal*, it means, as any child ought to know, precisely what *Tabal* meant before. Nothing more, nothing less. The word baptize, or *baptidzo*, then, in the Bible, has but one meaning—*purification*, or salvation from sin. Not the condition of salvation, as some stupidly confirm, but salvation itself."—Christian Baptism, pp. 10, 11.

Thus does this author dispose of the argument based upon the meaning of the word *baptizo* or *baptistheis*, in classic Greek. A Greek word in any other book, whatever its meaning, may mean something quite different the moment it is put into the Bible by a translator or writer. At least, that is the position of this writer as to the word *baptizo*, and if it is true of it, why not of other words?

Orpheus said (Argn. 5: 14): "But when the sun had dipped himself (original, baptized himself) into the flood of the ocean, and the dark-shining moon led in the stormy night, then went forth the war-like men who dwelt in the northern mountains."

And Heraclides Ponticus, "When a piece of iron is taken red hot from the fire, and is dipped (original, baptized) in water, the heat, being quenched by the peculiar nature of the water, ceases."—Scriptural Baptism, p. 17.

Here it is easy to see what the Greek word *baptizo* means, viz.: dip, plunge, immerse. None dispute that, but when "two hundred and eighty-five years before John the Baptist was born," when, according to Mr. Rogers, "the old Hebrew Scriptures were translated into Greek," and the action of Naaman, the leper, is described, and the translators wish to render into Greek the Hebrew word *taval* (spelled *tabal* by Mr. R.) they say: "And Naaman *ebaptizato en to Jordane.*"— See Scriptural Baptism, p. 45.

Mr. Rogers thinks it an "insult to *all* intelligence" to give the same meaning (dip, plunge, or immerse) to the same word. Pshaw! Some people's intelligence is very easily insulted. I wonder is it because of the quantity, and if so, is it large or small intelligences that are most easily insulted?

But for the argument's sake we will grant that Mr. Rogers' definition is correct and see how quickly his argument will explode in his own hands. Baptism, according to his rendering, means *in the Bible purification from sin* only. Let us now read, substituting purify or purification for baptize, baptism, etc.:

"I indeed have purified you with water, but he shall purify you with the Holy Ghost."— Mark 1: 8.

Mr. Rogers and others who believe with him may say it sounds all right, and that the "water of purity" (Num. 19) represented the blood of Christ just as our water of baptism does. (Chris. Bap., p. 12). And so John was simply sprinkling the water of purity on the people and promised them another baptism by the Christ when he came. But wait a minute: Does Mr. Rogers "purify" by sprinkling "the water of baptism" on those who are yet to be "purified" with the Holy Ghost? Does he not "purify" those who claim to have been already purified by this Holy Comforter? Why change the order and refuse to baptize with water until after the candidate has been already baptized with the Spirit?

"John verily baptized with the baptism of repentance" (Acts 19: 4), "unto repentance" (Matt. 3: 11), or in other words baptized *en* water those who repented or "brought forth fruits meet for repentance," or in other words, gave evidence of a genuine repentance and in this way gave "knowledge of salvation unto his people by the remission of sins." (Luke 1: 77). And then seeing they had believed his message and repented of their sins and were baptized of him *en, i. e. in* water for the remission of sins, John could very appropriately promise them: "He *shall* baptize you with the Holy Ghost."

But Mr. Rogers and his ilk do not like John. They wait until the people, in their judgment, *have been* baptized with the Holy Spirit and then sprinkle a little water upon them to "represent the work of grace in the soul." Such a practice is clearly at variance with that of John and so it cannot be the more excellent way.

Again:

"Then cometh Jesus from Galilee to Jordan unto John to be *purified* of him."—Matt. 3: 13.

What! Jesus Christ purified? From what? Sin? No; for he was "without sin." Neither was "guile found in his mouth." From what else could one need to be "purified?" Echo answers, What else? Jesus then was a sinner and needed purification, or cleansing, or saving or else Mr. Rogers' definition of *baptidzo* is wrong.

But Mr. Rogers claims that it is the spiritual baptism that saves. He also claims that the spiritual baptism has a "sign" or symbol and says: "The one saves *really* and the other emblematically." (Christian Baptism, p. 12).

The baptism of Jesus by John in the river of Jordan, then, was a sign or symbol or emblem of something that had taken place or was yet to take place. Mr. Rogers would have us to believe that it "represents the Spirit's work in our salvation." (Christian Baptism, p. 35). Then the Savior was a sinner and was saved by "the Spirit's work in his salvation" really, and was emblematically saved or "purified" by his baptism in Jordan at the hands of John. Can Mr. Rogers or any one else really be in earnest in professing to believe such an unreasonable and unscriptural proposition? If so, then I am sure they need to be "taught the way of God more perfectly," for they are not in "the more excellent way."

Again, if "*Baptidzo*" or baptize means to purify, then to purify means to baptize, and purification means baptism, etc.

Now let us read:

"Seeing ye have baptized [purified] your souls in obeying the truth through the Spirit, unto unfeigned love of the brethren, see that ye love one another with a pure heart fervently."—1 Pet. 1: 22.

Again:

"Cleanse your hands, ye sinners: and *baptize* [purify] your hearts, ye double minded."—James 4: 8.

Any one can see that the sense and true meaning of the above passages are destroyed by this way of defining and interpretation, hence no further proof is needed to show that Mr. Rogers' way of defining the word "*baptidzo*" is not the more excellent way. To believe Mr. Rogers is to believe that Christ was a sinner in reality and that the Holy Spirit's baptism saved him *really* and that his baptism in Jordan was a sign of the Spirit's baptism and saved him emblematically. It is difficult for the writer to see how persons with intelligences large enough to be "insulted" can possibly believe that.

To believe Mr. Rogers' theory is to believe that John the Baptist was wrong both as to design and the subjects of baptism, for,

"John verily baptized with the baptism of repentance, saying unto the people, that they should believe on him which should come after him, that is on Christ Jesus."—Acts 19: 4.

"I indeed have baptized you with water: but he [Christ] SHALL BAPTIZE you with the Holy Ghost."—Mark 1: 8.

That was John's way; Mr. Rogers reverses the order, waits until his candidate professes to receive the baptism of the Holy Ghost and then performs what he calls the rite of baptism with a few drops of water sprinkled upon the party *already* baptized, professedly, with the Holy Ghost. Any one can see that John's way and Mr. Rogers' way are opposed each to the other, that is, if his intelligence is not too badly "insulted" and I ask the reader to decide honestly as to which of the two is the more excellent way.

Again; John took his candidates down into the water, as seen in the baptism of Christ; he baptized them "in the river of Jordan" (see Mark 1: 5), and in so doing gave "remission of sins" (Luke 1: 77), and "knowledge of salvation" unto the people by such remission. This way of baptizing was accepted and submitted to by the Christ; was approbated by his Father, which approbation was clearly manifested by the Holy Ghost descending in the form of a dove and resting upon the Lord, while a voice from heaven—the voice of God—made known the fact that the work of John and Jesus was accepted by Him. Could there be a more excellent way to baptize than that?

Thus we see that God and Christ, and also the Holy Ghost, and John the Baptist are on record as approving immersion as the proper way to baptize, for the idea of baptizing "in the river of Jordan," the going down into the water and coming up out of the water, is unalterably opposed to the idea of baptism by any other method than immersion. And if any of my readers are yet unsatisfied and wish corroborative evidence, then I add to the list of witnesses the whole of that great multitude that went out from "Jerusalem, and all Judea, and all the region round about Jordan, and were baptized of him in Jordan, confessing their sins."—Matt. 3: 5, 6.

'Tis true we have no direct testimony in words from any of this multitude, but their action in submitting to the ordinance of baptism "in Jordan"—"in the river of Jordan," shows that their belief was immersion and not sprinkling or pouring. A man or a woman who is not willing to take the testimony of God the Father, and of Christ the Son, and of the Holy Ghost, corroborated by John, Philip, and as we have seen, by a whole multitude of people to whom John had given "knowledge of salvation by the remission of sins" by baptizing them for the remission of their sins, is entirely beyond the reach of evidence. To such an one evidence would be as pearls to swine. He would not believe one, nor a thousand, nor a million though they "arose from the dead."

Our case is proved with all upon whom evidence, borne either by human or divine witnesses, will have any effect. Others we know not how to reach. We give them over to the belief of their own traditions without proof; to the belief of the traditions and doctrines of men which have been substituted for the doctrine of Christ; but once more we wish to warn them, in the language of the wise man, that "There is a way that seemeth right unto a man, but the end thereof are the ways of death."—Prov. 14: 12.

Gently as the zephyrs of a calm May morning; yea, tender and sweet as the angelic song of "peace and good-will" at his birth, the voice of the Good Shepherd is heard, saying unto all:

"*I* am the way." "If any man serve me, let him follow *me;* and where I am, there shall also my servant be: * * * *him will my Father honour.*"—John 12: 26.

"Come unto me, all ye that labor and are heavy laden, and I will give you rest. Take *my* yoke upon you, and learn of *me;* * * * and ye' shall find rest to your souls."—Matt. 11: 28, 29.

Reader, do you wish to be honored of God? Do you wish to find rest to your soul? If so, then *follow* Christ in *all* things whatsoever he saith unto you, by precept or example, otherwise you "shall be destroyed from among the people" of God.

Now, if we really wish to follow Christ in this matter of baptism, what will we do?

First, as he went to John, a servant of God who had been sent to baptize with water, so we will go to one of God's servants who is authorized of God to baptize, "to be baptized of him."

Second, with this servant of God we will go down into the water in order to a proper baptism by immersion; otherwise how can we follow his example in "coming up straightway out of the water *when* he was baptized?"

God approved of this method of baptism and signified his approbation by sending his Spirit and acknowledging the divine Sonship of Him who received it. In like manner did he signify his approbation of this method of baptism in the case of Philip and the eunuch by sending his Spirit in such power that it "caught away Philip" and caused the eunuch to go "on his way rejoicing." Were not these persons honored of God the Father? Certainly. Well, then, the fact that God honored them is proof of the strongest character that they were following Christ—*the way*—"the more excellent way."

Are any of my readers hesitating still? Then I invite them to listen once more to that same gentle voice of the same Good Shepherd, and note that this time there is a tone of solemn warning in his voice:

"Verily, verily, I say unto you, He that entereth not by the door into the sheepfold, but climbeth up some other way, the same is a thief and a robber."—John 10:1.

Now, therefore, as our blessed Lord has taught us both by precept and example, yea, and by commandment (in that he saith, *"follow me"*), that the way to be baptized is by immersion and not by sprinkling or pouring, let us say in the language of Israel's sweet singer:

"Therefore I esteem *all* thy precepts concerning *all things* to be right; and I hate every false way."—Psa. 119:128.

God does not approve of false ways. Never at any time has he signified his approval of sprinkling or pouring by sending his Spirit upon those who were baptized in that way, as he did upon Jesus, John, Philip, and the eunuch. Not a line nor a verse can be found in the Bible showing that he did. But he did, as we have seen, approve, and signified his approval of immersion. Therefore I conclude that it is the more excellent way.

CHAPTER V.

Only a fractional part of the evidence or proof in favor of the necessity of baptism and the laying on of hands, and showing that they are a part of the more excellent way, has been pre-sented in the foregoing chapters; but, as stated before, enough has been given to prove our case with all who can be moved by the force of logical argument, based upon evidences of the strongest character, both human and divine.

But there are two questions still, in connection with baptism, to which we call attention, and to the answering of which this chapted is devoter.

1. By whom shall baptism be administered?

2. By whom shall it be re-ceived?

Here again, as elsewhere, in our search for the true way, we are invited by the worldly wise to walk in a number of different ways, and we are assured by the devotees of each that it is "the good way" in which we should walk, and that therein we may "find rest to our souls." But these ways do not agree; they do not lie along the same route, do not run in the same direction, and cannot all be right. From among them we must choose.

Then, dear reader, let us be careful to select the "more ex-cellent way."

As to who shall administer, not a great deal need be said, for since baptism is a heaven-or-dained and God-appointed ordi-nance, it stands to reason that no man could administer this holy rite, with acceptability to God, unless God had called him and authorized him so to do.

In Matthew 28:19, in address-ing his apostles, Jesus is made to say:

"Go ye therefore, and teach all nations, baptizing them in the name of the Father, and of the Son, and of the Holy Ghost."

For one party to do anything in the name of another party is to do it by the authority of that party. This is a well known and universally accepted principle, as applied to transactions be-tween men; why does it not hold good when applied to transactions between God and man? There is, indeed there can be, no good rea-son why it should not hold good. If then, the eleven apostles whom Jesus addressed in the words quoted above, were authorized to baptize "in the name of the Father, and of the Son, and of the Holy Ghost," it was because the Father, and the Son, and the

Holy Ghost had given them that authority; and without it they could not have baptized a single soul, in the sense in which the word is used in the commission. They might have immersed them, and that would have been a baptism so far as the classic meaning of the word is con-.cerned; but christian baptism—while, as we have seen, it cannot be administered by any other method than immersion—means more than immersion. It means immersion "in the name" or by the authority of the Father, Son, and Holy Ghost. Without such authority, immersion of itself considered, is not baptism; hence all those who have been immersed by unauthorized persons, *i. e.*, those not called of God, have not, in reality, been baptized in the sense the commission requires. They are right as to the manner, but wrong as to authority, and anything done without authority is not really done at all.

Illustration: A. sells a parcel of land, to which he holds legal title, to B. C., a regularly appointed and properly commissioned notary public, is called in to write the deed and take the acknowledgements of A. and his wife to the same. The deed is signed by A. and wife; the acknowledgements are taken according to law; the notary public certifies to the same, and affixes his seal; one or more witnesses attest the proceedings; the deed is delivered to B. and he is in full possession of the title to the land.

Again: D. sells a parcel of land to E., and F., who is in need of a little money, hears of the transaction and offers to write the deed and take the acknowledgements of D. and wife to the same. F. has no commission as a notary public, magistrate or other officer, but neither D. nor E. are aware of the fact, or if they are their questionings are soon silenced by the smooth words of F., and his assurances that he can write a deed that will answer as well as if written and acknowledged by C. or any other notary public; and they employ him to do the work. The deed is written, signed, acknowledged; F. adds his certificate, but affixes no seal, for he has none, which fact shows that he has no authority. The deed is then delivered to E., who goes home in fancied, but not in real, possession of the title to the land. Result: On test examination the deed is found to be of no value, because of F's lack of authority. E., therefore, has no real title, hence he cannot legally hold it nor convey it to any other party. D. must go to the trouble and expense of making another deed.

Meanwhile F. is arrested and punished for violation of the law of the land for presuming to do what he was not, under the law, commissioned to do.

Now everyone knows this to be true, and every one knows that it is right that it should be true. It is necessary for the protection of the rights of men. Now, do any of my readers think it is right for the law of the land to punish those who act without authority in earthly matters and at the same time think it right for any one who is presumptuous enough to do so, to step right over into the sacred realms of the kingdom of God and proceed, without proper authority, to administer the laws and sacred ordinances of the same? Surely not. No one with reasonable judgment could be so inconsistent.

The eleven apostles were authorized to baptize. No one will dispute that. Now, who else?

"There was a man sent from God whose name was John."—John 1: 6.

Now read verse 33:

"And I knew him not: but he that sent me to baptize with water, the same said unto me, Upon whom thou shalt see the Spirit descending, and remaining on him, the same is he which baptizeth with the Holy Ghost."

This scripture shows, (1) that John the Baptist, was sent from God, and that (2) he was sent to "baptize with water." No room for any doubt that he had authority to baptize, and it was the very best authority—the authority of God himself. This is further attested by the fact that Jesus went to John for baptism. He knew John's baptism was all right, that it was from heaven and not of men.

"And Jesus answered and said unto them, I also will ask you one thing, which if ye tell me, I in likewise will tell you by what authority I do these things. The baptism of John, whence was it? from heaven, or of men? And they reasoned with themselves, saying, If we shall say, From heaven; he will say unto us, Why did ye not then believe him?"—Matt. 21: 24. 25.

The above verses show that Christ recognized that John's baptism was from heaven, for he virtually confesses to the chief priests that his authority to do these things was from the same source as John's baptism, or authority to baptize. It was a very logical conclusion that these chief priests and elders came to, when they reasoned that, "If we shall say from heaven, he will say unto us, Why did ye not then believe him?" If he had received authority from men they would not have been under any obligation to receive baptism at his hands. Nor are we today under any obligation to receive baptism at the hands of any man who has not been authorized of God, i. e. called and commissioned of God to baptize.

"But," says one, "Jesus says,

o ye into all the world, and preach the gospel to every creature.' (Mark 16: 15). That is our authority to preach; and again he says, 'Go ye therefore, and teach all nations, baptizing them' etc. That is our authority to teach and baptize."

Yes, I have read that he said that; but did he say it to you? Did he say it to any of the reformers and church builders, such as Luther, Calvin, Knox, Henry VIII, Wesley, Campbell or Ellen G. White, or any one else?

"O yes," says one, "he says so to them through the Bible, but not by revelation direct." And they went out on the authority of the words of Jesus to eleven apostles, but not to themselves, and preached, baptized, and builded churches? "Yes," and the words "go ye" are to be applied to every man who chooses or "feels impressed" to go? "Yes." Then the commission, though given to the eleven apostles, may be used by any one who chooses to apply it to himself, and by the authority of the words "go ye" he may go out and preach and baptize? "Yes."

Well now, reader, if you insist that the commission to the apostles, as given by Matthew and Mark is applicable to men today in clothing them with authority to preach and baptize, may I just ask if the same commission to the same eleven apostles as recorded by Luke is also applicable? And, of course, to this question you must answer yes.

Now read:

"And ye are witnesses of these things. And, behold, I send the promise of my Father upon you: but tarry ye in the city of Jerusalem, until ye be endued with power from on high."—Luke 24: 48, 49.

Now if "go ye" in Matthew and Mark is applicable to any man today, then we insist that, "tarry ye," in Luke, is equally applicable and must be heeded, or there will be no validity attaching to the ministry and baptism of any one who fails to "tarry" at Jerusalem or some other place until he is "endued with power from on high" and not from the faculty of some theological seminary.

The commission to the apostles does not, and cannot authorize any man now living to preach or to baptize, unless some of them are now living, and if they are, their commission does not authorize anybody outside of the eleven, to either preach or baptize, any more than Noah's commission to build an ark authorizes them to build another ark, or Moses' commission to lead the Israelites out of Egyptian bondage authorizes them to lead the Jews from Russia over into Palestine today.

When God wanted John to preach and baptize he called and sent him to the work. When Jesus wanted the apostles to go and preach and baptize, he knew that John's commission, though it was from heaven, was not sufficient for them, and so he gave them a commission for themselves. When he wanted a quorum of seventy, he "appointed" and sent them saying, "Go your ways." (Luke 10:3). When he wanted Paul and Barnabas he called them by the Holy Ghost, speaking through the prophets at Antioch, and they were "sent forth by the Holy Ghost." (Acts 13:3, 4). When he wanted elders they were called by the Holy Ghost, and by it they were made overseers over the flocks of God. (Acts 20:28).

For none of these, nor for any other minister for God of which the Bible makes mention, would any former commission to some other party answer; but every-one must and did have a call and commission for himself, and that by revelation from God either directly or indirectly. Such were authorized to baptize; none others were. Such are authorized to baptize today; none others are.

"Hard on those who do not believe in present revelation," did you say? "Friend, I do thee no wrong." Did you not agree to take the "tarry ye" in Luke, as well as the "go ye" in Matthew? The fact that God approved of baptisms that were performed by those whom he called, such as John (Matt. 3), the eleven (Mark 16: 20, Acts 2: 38), Paul (Acts 19), Philip (Acts 8), is of itself strong proof that the position for which we are now contending is true, viz., that only those who are called of God are authorized to baptize in his name. These are they who may be likened unto the true notary who had authority to make deeds and take acknowledgements thereof and convey title, even the remission of sin. Who could wish for a more excellent way than that?

Reader, did you know that in our times, just as in times of old, baptisms are being performed that are approved of God by the giving of his Spirit, attesting the fact that sins have been remitted, that pardon has been received?

Do you not know further that in these days, just as in days of old, there are thousands of so-called baptisms, sprinklings, pourings, and even immersions, without authority; which God does not recognize or approve by sending his Spirit upon those who administer, or those who receive them? Such administrators may be likened unto the notary who makes deeds and acknowledges without any commission, and hence cannot convey title; and those who receive such baptisms, if it were proper to call them such, are in the same condition as the parties who were deceived by the fraudulent work of the pretended notary who had no commission and no seal with which to attest and make good his work. No one ought to mistake that for the more excellent way, yet many do and are seemingly satisfied without the approval of God's Spirit bearing witness with their spirit that they are the children of God and have a right or title properly conveyed by the authority of God, securing to them a home in the land of peace. Is it not strange that that should be mistaken for the more excellent way?

SUBJECTS OF BAPTISM.

Let us take up now the second question referred to at the beginning of this chapter, viz.,

Who are proper subjects of baptism, or by whom should baptism be received?

One party says those of mature age, who have already received the baptism of the Holy Ghost, and been made new creatures in Christ Jesus.

Another party says that little children—infants—are proper subjects of baptism as well as those of mature age, who have previously been baptized of the Spirit.

And still another party says: "Penitent believers, whose sins are not yet forgiven, are to be baptized for the remission of sins."

Possibly there are other views entertained, but this will suffice for our present purpose. Here are three ways of looking at this question and as they are different, essentially so, they cannot all be right. All are not in harmony with the teaching of Him who said, "I am the way."

Let us look at this first position, that is that those of mature age who have been baptized with the Holy Ghost are the only proper subjects of water baptism. The writer agrees with the party making this claim so far as relates to those of mature age, at least sufficiently mature to be taught the principles of the gospel, of which baptism is one; but he disagrees with them in that only those who have previously been baptized of the Spirit are fit subjects for water baptism.

In these articles scriptural evidences have been adduced in great abundance to show that John baptized *sinners;* people who confessed their sins, and *after* he had baptized them with water, he promised them they should yet receive the Holy Ghost. (See Mark 1: 8). If these people had received the Holy Ghost, John did not know it, and yet he had baptized them: or if he did know, he promised that they should receive, sometime in the future, that which they already had received, and were still in possession of at that time. To believe John did that, is to believe him to have been knavish or foolish, or both. We can hardly afford to do that.

Again: The Samaritans were baptized in water by Philip, but had not yet received the baptism of the Holy Ghost. The apostles heard of their baptism, and sent Peter and John, "Who, when they were come down, prayed for them, *that they might receive the Holy Ghost:* for as yet he was fallen upon *none* of them: only they were baptized in the name of the Lord Jesus."—Acts 8: 15, 16.

To say that none are entitled to water baptism only those who have already received the Holy Ghost, is to dispute the foregoing verses of Scripture; and to say that Philip made a mistake, that Peter and John also made a mistake, and that the rest of the apostles at Jerusalem were compromised in the mistake with them is unwarranted by the facts and, worst of all, it is to say that God sanctioned the mistake; for the 17th verse says:

"Then laid they [Peter and John] their hands on them and they [people who had been baptized in water] received the Holy Ghost."

Now, we have two positions before us, either one of which we may accept.

1. That God, the Holy Ghost, Peter, John, the rest of the apostles at Jerusalem, and Philip all made a mistake in teaching that persons who had *not* received the Holy Spirit or its baptism, were proper subjects for baptism in water, or

2. Those who now teach that only those who have received the Holy Ghost, or its baptism, are entitled to water baptism, are making a mistake in so teaching. To believe the former is to at once destroy the foundation of all religion so far as Bible revealments are concerned. To believe the latter therefore is certainly the more excellent way to dispose of this matter. It is better for us to enter into life with no human creed, yea, with all creeds (except the creed of Christ) blotted out of existence, than to have a hundred, or a thousand, creeds, and, with them, be cast "into outer darkness, where there shall be weeping and wailing and gnashing of teeth."

Again: On the day of Pentecost a vast number were convinced by the powerful discourse of Peter, insomuch that they

"Said unto Peter and to the rest of the apostles, Men and brethren, what shall we do?"—Acts 2: 37.

There's an important question; and the answer, as given in the Good Book, throws light on the question, who shall be baptized? Let us read it, v. 38:

"Then Peter said unto them, Repent, and be baptized, every one of you, in the name of Jesus Christ for the remission of sins, and ye shall receive the gift of the Holy Ghost."

That was *Peter's* answer. It was the answer of "the rest of the apostles," for they stood up with him and not one of them demurred or objected, or excepted to his answer, and that compromises them again. It was the answer of the Holy Ghost, for Peter and his brethren were filled with it at the time, and "spake with tongues as the Spirit gave them utterance." (Verse 4). It was the answer of Jesus Christ, Peter says:

"This Jesus hath God raised up whereof we all are witnesses. Therefore being by the right hand of God, exalted, and having received of the Father the promise of the Holy Ghost, *he hath shed forth this,* which ye now see and hear."—v. 33.

It was the answer of God, the Father, for in verses 16 and 17 we read:

"But this is that which was spoken by the prophet Joel; And it shall come to pass in the last days, *saith God, I* will pour out *my Spirit* upon all flesh," etc.

Now, if God poured out his Spirit on Peter and others as is here declared, then whatever Peter said under the power of that Spirit was the voice of God's Spirit, therefore the voice of God himself. So it is easy to see that God sanctioned or approved the answer of Peter.

Now let us sum up the question and the answer.

1. People who have received neither the baptism of water, nor the baptism of the Spirit, but who are sinners, and in a sense the slayers of Christ (v. 37), ask, "What shall we do?"

2. In answer they are told (a) to repent, (b) to be baptized, and (c) ye [who repent and are baptized] *shall* [future tense] receive the gift of the Holy Ghost.

Any one can see that according to this answer the baptism of water preceded the baptism of the Spirit, just as when John baptized the multitudes in Jordan, and when Philip baptized the denizens of Samaria.

Who are the witnesses to this order, and how many are there? (1), We write Peter's name on the list as he is spokesman. Then we write (2) Andrew, (3) James, son of Zebedee, (4) John, (5) Philip, (6) Bartholomew, (7) Thomas, (8) Matthew, (9) James, son of Alpheus, (10) Lebeus, (11) Simon, (12) Matthias. These are the names of the quorum of the Twelve, and they stand as a unit upon this matter. John the Baptist baptized persons in water who had not yet had the baptism of the Spirit (Mark 1: 8), and so we write him as our thirteenth witness that water baptism precedes Holy Ghost baptism. Philip, the evangelist, as we have seen, did the same thing at Samaria, so we write him down as the fourteenth, and Paul did the same thing at Ephesus (Acts 19: 1-4), so he makes the fifteenth; while the Holy Ghost came to different ones at different times, who had previously been baptized in water, hence we may safely write him as the sixteenth witness. Jesus Christ, as we have seen, did, on the day of Pentecost, "shed forth" those wonderful things which were done and said, thus signifying his approval and we unhesitatingly write Him as our seventeenth witness. And as God the Father, sent or "poured out" his Spirit upon those who taught and those who accepted the doctrine that water baptism precedes Spirit baptism, with confidence we write Him as our eighteenth witness in the case of the matter before us.

Eighteen witnesses, especially when three of them speak directly from heaven, and the others are in good standing and of good repute as members of the kingdom of God on earth, ought to be sufficient to prove any cause. There can be no doubt that they all agree, that their testimony is all on one side, and in favor of the idea that penitent persons may receive baptism in water previous to the baptism of the Holy Ghost. On the strength of this evidence we rest our case, confident in the belief that our way is more excellent than any other, because it is God's way; and that the idea that *only* those who have received the Spirit's baptism are entitled to the baptism of water, is not "the good way" because it is "not cast up" by the Lord.

But are there no witnesses on the other side; are there none who answer the question, "What shall we do," in a different way than did these eighteen witnesses?

Yes, plenty of them. Friend, if you are on the other side of the question, you are not by yourself by any means. Millions of people, including great and mighty Doctors of Divinity, testify for you and say that no one is entitled to water baptism until he has been baptized of the Spirit.

"Well, then, have I not the advantage in the number of witnesses," do you ask?

Yes, as to *numbers* you do have the advantage; but as to character, credibility or reliability of witnesses, how is it? Is not the advantage with the eighteen witnesses who are against you? Yea, verily. Surely nothing more need be said on that point.

INFANT BAPTISM.

A little time and space devoted to the question, "Are infants proper subjects of water baptism?'' and we are done.

What we have already presented proves clearly that they are
not, for they are not sinners, and
as already proved, water baptism
is for repentant sinners; and as
infants are not sinners—and if
they were, would be utterly incapable of repentance—baptism
is not intended for them. That
is reason enough why infants
need not to be baptized; but hear
Mr. A. F. Rogers tell why they
should be:

"I claim that infants (children)
are proper subjects; that God *requires* it; that we have scripture
example for it; that if we withhold
it we are guilty of violating *posi-
tive* law; and that in thus with-
holding it we deny their interest
in Christ and their title to heaven.
* * * If infants are saved they
must be baptized, for there is no
salvation without it. Not that
they cannot be saved in heaven
without *water* baptism. I say no
such thing. But I do say, that
if they are saved in heaven the
only thing in the universe that
*saves them is the baptism of the Holy
Ghost*, of which water baptism is
the sign."—Christian Baptism,
pp. 71, 72. (Last emphasis mine).

Again:

"But if Christ saves them, it
is from sin; and what sin have
they to be saved from? Guilt?
No; they have none to be pardoned. There is, therefore, but
one sense in which he can save
them, and that is from the *de-*

*pravity of their nature that unfits
them for heaven.*''—p. 73. (Emphasis mine).

On page 74 he says: "The uni-
versal necessity of the new birth
arises from the fact that we all
have been 'born of the flesh'—
that is of sinful parents; consequently we have a sinful nature, for 'like can only produce
like.' ''

Further along on same page:
"Our infant children, then, need
and must have both the sign and
the thing signified (water and
Spirit baptism), for they are born
of the flesh even as we, and without the birth or baptism of the
Spirit *they cannot be saved.*'' (Emphasis mine).

Mr. Rogers' position is now
pretty clearly set forth.

1st. Infants come into the
world totally depraved, or at
least with a depravity of nature
that unfits them for heaven.

2d. This depravity of their
nature must be taken away by
the baptism of the Spirit or *"they
cannot be saved."*

3d. Mr. Rogers assumes without one scintilla of evidence to
support him in the assumption
and not a syllable of proof does
he even try to offer in its support that water baptism is a
"sign" of the Spirit's baptism,
and must be given to infants by
the minister *because* it is sup-
posed that God has *saved* the
poor infants from that "depravity of their nature that unfits

them for heaven;" hence he concludes that infants need and *must* have the "sign."

But Mr. Rogers' premise is wrong to start with; his conclusion must be wrong also.

Webster defines "depraved:" *Corrupt*, wicked, destitute of holiness or good principles.

"Totally" he defines thus: Wholly, entirely, fully, completely.

If, then, infants come into the world in a totally depraved state, they are born wholly corrupt, entirely wicked, completely destitute of holiness or good principles; can any sane man believe that?

Calvin's doctrine that:

"Reprobate infants are vipers of vengeance which God holds over the flames of hell, until they turn and spit venom in God's face" (See Calvin's Institutes, Vol. 1; *Saints' Herald*, Sept. 5, 1900), is no worse.

"But," says one, "the Bible does not say anything about *reprobate* infants." Very true; but it says fully as much about reprobate infants as it does about infants that are totally *depraved*, wholly wicked, entirely corrupt. The devil himself is not worse than that.

Now, having seen what Mr. Rogers and Mr. Calvin believe about the condition of infants at birth, let us see what Jesus taught respecting them:

"But Jesus said, Suffer little children, and forbid them not, to come unto me: for of *such* is the kingdom of heaven."—Matt. 19: 14.

Again:

"And said, Verily I say unto you, Except ye be converted and become as little children, ye shall not enter into the kingdom of heaven."—Matt. 18: 3.

This scripture shows that Jesus regarded that the character of infants—"little children," is exactly the kind that men must have in order to enter into and inherit the kingdom of heaven. Jesus was right; and if Mr. Rogers was right in his claim that infants have a "depravity of nature that unfits them for heaven," and if Mr. Calvin was right in his claim that infants—some of them at least—"are vipers of vengeance," then for us to "be converted and become as little children" and consequently fit to enter and abide in the kingdom of heaven, we would have to become "totally depraved;" that is, we must become "wholly corrupt," "entirely wicked" and "completely destitute of holiness," or to use Calvin's words, we must become "vipers of vengeance" in order to enter into the kingdom of heaven. Nonsensical as this appears, we must believe it or discard the heresy upon which Mr. Rogers bases his argument in favor of infant baptism, viz., that children are born into the world with "a depravity of nature that unfits them for heaven," and that "without the birth or baptism of the Spirit they cannot be saved."

But Mr. Rogers does not bebelieve this heresy himself. In fact, no man of sound judgment can believe it unless he refuses to use his judgment. •After taking the ground, as the quotations already given from his little book show, that "the only thing in the universe that saves them [infants] is the baptism of the Holy Ghost," and that to withhold water baptism from infants is to "deny their interest in Christ and their title to heaven," and that the baptism of the Spirit saves them from "that depravity of their nature *that unfits them for heaven*," and that our infant children * * * are born of the flesh even as we, and without the birth or baptism of the Spirit they *cannot be saved*"—after proclaiming this monstrous heresy with as great a flourish of trumpets as Joshua's priests did when they encompassed the city of Jericho —there seems to have been a mutiny of his stifled conscience, a revolution of his misguided and mistreated judgment until finally, in spite of himself, he "flops" and explodes his own arguments by contradicting himself thus, page 78:

"Here, then, is infantile justification. Christ purchased the blessing and the Holy Ghost applied, and our infants came into the world in this state of grace— *children of God and heirs of glory.* Many of them die and *go to glory before they ever see the light of this world,*" etc. (Emphasis mine).

Now, if our infants come into this world children of God, heirs of glory, then I am much puzzled to know how they came with "a depravity of nature that unfits them for heaven." If *many* of them die and go to glory before they ever see the light of this word," I am at a loss to know why they "*need* and *must have*" both the baptism of water and Spirit and why without the latter "they cannot be saved." Does God "baptize their souls" before they are born? If so, then they are not born totally depraved are they? Or do they "backslide" in their pre-natal state so that they "need" the baptism of water and of the Spirit that they may be saved?

If God does baptize their souls before birth, neither Mr. Rogers nor any other man knows anything about it, for there is no revelation of the fact in the Bible or elsewhere. If God ever baptized the soul of a single infant since the world began and by that baptism saved that soul "from that depravity of nature" that unfitted it for heaven, then he has kept it a profound secret; for there is not one line, sentence, word or syllable of revelation in regard to it. Mr. Rogers simply assumes it, but does not prove nor even attempt to prove it. Why is this? Echo answers, Why?

But there is no need for me to say more. Mr. Rogers has, as we have seen, blown up his own magazine and bursted his only gun. He bases his whole argument on the depravity of infants and their consequent *need* of the Spirit's baptism, and then overthrows his position by admitting that they come into the world in a state of grace—"children of God and heirs of glory."

Baptism in water is "for the remission of sin." Infants have no sins to remit. Therefore infant baptism is not a part of the more excellent way.

Baptism in water is for those who believe (Mark 16: 16; Acts 8: 37), and for those who repent (Acts 2: 38). Infants can neither believe nor repent; therefore infant baptism is no part of the more excellent way.

"Go ye therefore and teach all nations, baptizing *them* in the name of the Father, and of the Son, and of the Holy Ghost."— Jesus to the eleven, Matt. 28: 19.

They were to baptize those whom they *taught*. Infants cannot be taught, hence there neither was nor is a commission to baptize them; therefore infant baptism is no part of the more excellent way.

Suffer little children, and forbid them not, to come unto me: for of such is the kingdom of heaven. And he laid his hands on them and departed thence."— Matt. 19: 14, 15.

"And he took them up in his arms, put his hands upon them, and blessed them."—Mark 10: 16.

That *is* the more excellent way, for it is according to the mind of him who said: "I AM THE WAY."

It is not pretended that anything like an exhaustive discussion of matters presented in this paper has been made, but it is hoped that at least a few rays of light have been thrown across the path of some who may be in search of the more, yea, the most excellent way—"*the good way*"— and may they be able to find it and "walk therein," and so doing "find rest to their souls."